Ribbonwork *Gardens*

The Ultimate Visual Guide to 122 Flowers, Leaves & Embellishment Extras

Christen Brown

C&T PUBLISHING

Photography and Artwork copyright © 2012 by C&T Publishing, Inc.

Publisher: Amy Marson

Creative Director: Gailen Runge

Art Director/Cover Designer: Kristy Zacharias

Editor: Liz Aneloski

Technical Editors: Janice Wray and Gailen Runge

Book Designer: Christina Jarumay Fox

Production Coordinator: Jenny Davis

Production Editor: Alice Mace Nakanishi

Gallery Photography by Christina Carty-Francis and Diane Pedersen of C&T Publishing, Inc., unless otherwise noted

How-To Photography by Christen Brown

Published by C&T Publishing, Inc., P.O. Box 1456, Lafayette, CA 94549

Library of Congress Cataloging-in-Publication Data

Brown, Christen (Christen Joan)
 Ribbonwork gardens : the ultimate visual guide to 122 flowers, leaves & embellishment extras / Christen Brown.
    p. cm.
 ISBN 978-1-60705-412-2 (soft cover)
 1. Ribbon work. 2. Ribbon flowers. 3. Silk ribbon embroidery. I. Title.
 TT850.5.B76 2012
 677'.76--dc23

                    2011037258

Printed in China
10 9 8 7 6 5 4 3 2 1

HAPPY CREATING

*I dedicate this book to all of my students,
both past and present.
Thank you for giving me this opportunity
to share my knowledge with you.
May you always find the time
to enjoy the creative adventure.*

With love, Christen

SPECIAL THANKS

*To my father-in-law, Richard,
for allowing me to see the flowers,
one petal at a time.*

*To my friend Maryanne,
for checking my directions
to make sure I didn't mess it all up!*

WITH ALL MY LOVE

*To my husband, Kevin, and daughter, Gwen,
my two biggest fans, for your unconditional love and support
and for letting me play in my room.*

CONTENTS

the flowers, leaves, and extras

VISUAL GUIDE

ESSENTIAL GARDENS ... 33

Rosette · 35

Folded-Edge Posy · 40

Spiral-Loop Petals · 45

Double-Edge Rosette · 36

Folded Petals · 41

Bias-Loop Petals · 46

Folded-Edge Rosette · 37

Two-Petal Flower · 42

Ruched Petals · 47

Posy · 38

U-Gather Petals · 43

Individual-Petal Flower · 48

Double-Edge Posy · 39

Shutterbug Petals · 44

COTTAGE GARDENS ... 49

Single Peony · 51

Gillyflower · 56

Triple Delight · 61

Daffodil · 52

Lady's Bonnet · 57

Dandelion · 62

Viola · 53

Marigold · 58

Cottage Sunflower · 63

Trillium · 54

Snapdragon · 59

Delphinium · 55

Lady's Slipper · 60

URBAN GARDENS ... 64

Chrysanthemum 66

Veronica 72

Carnation 67

Geranium 73

Black-Eyed Susan 68

Decorative Dahlia 74

Forget-Me-Nots 68

Ranunculus 75

Clematis 69

Azalea 76

Dianthus 70

Anemone 77

Wood Orchid 71

GRANDMOTHERS' GARDENS ... 78

Crocus 80

Aster 86

Narcissus 81

Vine Flower 87

Maid's Cap 82

Mallow 88

Cathedral Bells 83

Camellia 89

Hollyhock 84

Coneflower 90

Sweet Pea 85

Bearded Iris 91

ENCHANTED GARDENS ... 93

Begonia 95

Bleeding Heart 101

Pansy 96

Orchid 102

Lupine 97

Persian Violet 103

Morning Glory 98

Fuchsia 104

Star Lily 99

Cosmos 105

Zinnia 100

Jasmine 106

ROSES, QUEENS OF THE GARDEN ... 107   PETALS AND GREENERY ... 120

Lingerie Rose

Primrose

Couture Leaf, Petal, or Bud; and Knot Center

Triangle-Fold Leaf, Petal, or Bud

Fleur-de-Lis Leaf

Victorian Leaf

Victorian Rose

Tea Rose

Lazy Loop Leaf, Petal, or Bud

Elizabethan Leaf, Petal, or Bud

Lance Leaf

Jester's Leaf

Ramblin' Rose

Shy Rose

Parisian Leaf, Petal, or Bud

Simple Leaf, Petal, or Bud

Spanish Leaf

Iris Leaf

Vintage Rose

Floribunda Rose

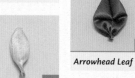
Pinwheel Leaf, Petal, or Bud

Spear-Tip Leaf, Petal, or Bud

Arrowhead Leaf

Majestic Leaf

Gypsy Rose

Elegant Rose

Kimono Leaf, Petal, or Bud

Lollypop Leaf

Teardrop Leaf

Thin Leaf

Edwardian Leaf

Triple Spear-Tip Leaf

GARDEN EXTRAS ... 139

133 Crown Leaf

136 Simple Calyx

140 Country Heart

143 Summer's Dragonfly

147 Elegant Heart

134 Twin Elizabethan Leaf

137 Morning Glory Leaf

140 Fan

144 Shutterbug Center and Button

148 Looped Plume

134 Twin Lazy Loop Leaf

137 Rounded Leaf

141 Double Fan

145 Simple Bow

148 Half U-Gather Petals

135 Regal Leaf

138 Double-Edge Leaf

141 Garden Snail

145 Ribbon Button

149 Woven and Silk Bias Berries

135 Kimono Calyx and Bud

138 Pointed Leaf

142 Gwen's Butterfly

146 Shy Butterfly

136 Bud Cap

Welcome to
My Flower Garden

Rococo Pillow, 6¾" × 7". Ribbonworked flowers stitched to silk background with silk ribbon embroidery

Introduction

I have been fond of flowers and gardens all of my life, marveling at the variety in each unique burst of color and at the little quiet surprises that peep out of the earth. In the summers of my youth I wandered through the truly enchanted garden of my grand-parents' backyard and the lake country wildflowers that surrounded our cottage.

Ribbonwork Gardens was written as a reference guide for you, the creative reader who wishes to expand your artistic horizons. The stylized and truly dimensional, lifelike examples of ribbonworked flowers, leaves, and garden extras are made from a variety of ribbons, construction techniques, and embellishments.

Ribbonwork and Ribbon Embroidery

I often find that ribbonwork is confused with ribbon embroidery, possibly because both mediums use a ribbon and a needle to create a flower or leaf. I offer the definitions and samples below as a simple explanation of the differences between the two.

Ribbonwork is stitching a length of ribbon with needle and thread to form a flower, leaf, or other design as a separate, individual unit.

Sweetheart, 3¼" × 3". The embroidery on this brooch was stitched with 4mm and 7mm silk embroidery ribbon.

Vintage Bib, 6¼" × 6½". The flowers and leaves stitched to this crochet bib are handmade from silk bias ribbon.

Ribbon embroidery is threading the needle with the ribbon and stitching through fabric to form a flower, leaf, or other design, which enhances the surface of the fabric.

Flowers, Leaves, and Garden Extras

The flowers in this book are listed in chapters that identify where they may be found in a garden setting, but this does not suggest that a flower cannot be used or grouped with one from another chapter. The flower and leaf combinations can be mingled with a variety of buds and garden extras to create your own floral vignettes.

Your Own Garden

It is important to remember that this is your garden and that you are the designer. The colors, sizes, and types of ribbons that I have used in the samples are only suggestions. I encourage you to use the techniques included in this book to enhance your own personal body of knowledge and to use the gallery of suggestions to ignite your artistic spirit.

Ribbons, Glorious Ribbons

Group of ribbons

Ribbon Properties

Each project in this book will list the suggested type of ribbon best suited for the ribbonwork technique or design. The assembly may depend on the specific qualities of the ribbon, including the fiber content, the hand, the patterning, and the edge of the ribbon.

HAND

The thickness, weave, fiber content, and patterning of the ribbon determine its *hand*, which is described as soft, medium, or stiff. As a general guideline, soft ribbons are best suited for a design that is gathered into shape, whereas medium to stiff ribbons work best for a flower that has cut and folded or looped and individually formed petals.

PATTERNING

Patterning refers to the variety of colors woven into the ribbon or a print applied to the surface of the ribbon.

Ombré and Variegated Ribbons

Ombré and variegated ribbons have a blend of color across their width, although a ribbon could also change colors along its length. An ombré ribbon is a blend of one color from a darker to lighter shade, such as red to pink; a variegated ribbon is a blend of two or more colors, such as peach to fuchsia to olive.

Embroidered, Textured, or Printed Surface Designs

Sometimes ribbon is woven in an intricate pattern that leaves a design on one side. Other patterns that produce a ribbon with a right and wrong side include pleats, textures, and printed designs that are applied after the ribbon is woven.

Types of Ribbon

The three types of ribbon used to create the ribbon-work designs in this book are woven, wire-edge, and silk bias ribbons. Woven ribbons come in both natural and synthetic fibers; wire-edge ribbons are made from synthetic fibers. Silk bias ribbons are made from silk fabric cut on the bias.

WOVEN RIBBONS

Woven ribbons come in a variety of weaves, textures, surfaces, and hands; all have finished selvage edges.

Double-Sided Satin Ribbons

Double-sided satin comes with the shiny finish on both sides and sometimes a different color on each side. The hand can be medium to stiff, and the fiber content can be synthetic or silk. For this ribbon, choose a design with formed petals in which one or both sides of the ribbon will show.

Clematis made from double-sided satin ribbon

Grosgrain Ribbons

Grosgrain ribbons are woven with a pattern of raised ribs of thread that run across the width of the ribbon. The hand is usually medium to stiff, and the fiber content is cotton or synthetic. Choose a design with formed petals in which one or both sides of the ribbon will show.

Gillyflower made from vintage cotton grosgrain ribbon

Jacquard Ribbons

Jacquard refers to a complex overshot pattern of threads that are woven to resemble embroidery on the right side of the ribbon. The hand is usually stiff, and the fiber content is cotton, synthetic, or a combination of fibers. Choose a design with formed petals in which only one side of the ribbon will show.

Shutterbug Petal flower made from jacquard ribbon

Spring Pansy Bracelet, 1" × 6¾"

Novelty Ribbons

Novelty ribbons, such as satin ribbons with a picot edge or taffeta ribbons with a ruffled edge, need to be oriented with the embellishment toward the outer edge of the design. A woven ribbon with a pleated, folded, or textured surface has a right and wrong side. The hand can be medium to stiff, and the fiber content can be cotton, synthetic, or a combination. Choose a design in which only one edge or one side of the ribbon will show.

Double-Edge Rosette made from ribbon with a ruffled edge

Sheer Ribbons

Organza, georgette, and organdy ribbons are fine, sheer, or opaque, often found with a shimmering or iridescent surface. The hand is extremely soft, and the fiber content is usually synthetic. Choose a design with gathering along the length, in which one or both sides of the ribbon will show.

Lingerie Rose made from sheer ribbon

Silk Habotai Ribbons

Silk habotai is a fine, loosely woven ribbon with a finished edge and a soft hand. Choose a design with gathered petals or center, in which one or both sides of the ribbon will show.

Snapdragon made from silk habotai ribbon

Single-Sided Satin Ribbons

Single-sided satin ribbon has one shiny side and one dull side. The hand can be soft, medium, or stiff, and the fiber content is synthetic or silk. Choose a design in which only one side of the ribbon will show.

U-Gather Petal flower made from single-sided satin ribbon

Sunflower Brooch, 2⅞" × 2¾"

Taffeta Ribbons

Taffeta ribbons have a fine, tight, even weave; often the warp and weft are different colors to create a changeable surface. The hand is medium, and the fiber content is usually synthetic. Choose a design with gathered or formed petals, in which one or both sides of the ribbon will show.

Pansy made from ombré taffeta ribbon

Velvet Ribbons

Velvet ribbons have a plush finish on one side and a dull finish on the other side. The hand is medium to stiff thick plush, and the fiber content is cotton, rayon, silk, or synthetic. Choose a design with formed petals in which one or both sides of the ribbon will show.

Lady's Bonnet made from velvet ribbon

WIRE-EDGE RIBBONS

French wire ribbon and wire-edge ribbon are usually fine, woven taffeta ribbons with a thin wire sewn through the woven edges. The hand is usually medium, and the fiber content is synthetic. Choose a design with formed petals in which one or both sides of the ribbon will show.

Trillium made from French wire ombré ribbon

The wire gives body and shape to the ribbon, making it excellent for most woven-ribbon projects. But the wire edge can be difficult to stitch. I suggest removing the wire on the edge that will be gathered; this will allow the stitches to gather evenly to create a smaller center.

However, in a folded technique, where both edges will be gathered, removing the wire will cause loss of body and shape. It may take some practice to create even stitches with the wire still in place.

Wire-edge ribbon

Craft Wire Ribbons

Craft wire ribbons come in a variety of textures, weaves, and prints and have a thicker wire sewn through the woven edges. The hand is very stiff, and the fiber content is synthetic. The texture, pattern, and fiber content of this ribbon may be best suited for use in a bow or loop.

SILK BIAS RIBBONS

Silk bias ribbons are cut on the bias from sewn silk habotai, silk satin, or silk velvet fabric; they have a raw edge along the width and a stitched seam about every two yards. The hand is extremely soft because of the silk fabric and pliable due to the bias cut. Choose a design with gathered petals or center, in which one or both sides of the ribbon will show.

Triple Delight made from silk bias ribbon

LAYERING RIBBON

You can create your own unique ribbons by combining different sizes and types.

Layer and pin a narrower-width ribbon along the selvage of a wider-width ribbon. Stitch both layers of ribbon at the same time.

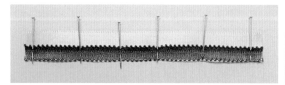

Ribbon layers pinned together

Carnation made from layered ribbons

Ribbon Care

In order for your ribbonwork designs to look their best, the ribbon you begin with should be dust- and wrinkle-free. Test the colorfastness of the ribbon if you plan to wash the finished piece.

STORAGE

Store your ribbon in a plastic bin and wrapped on the original cardboard spool (remove any tape that may be attached to the raw edges) or on a cardboard tube. You can also wrap the ribbon in a loop or a figure-eight bundle and store it in a plastic bag with a zipper closure. Do not secure ribbon with a straight pin, which will damage the weave; likewise, twist ties or rubber bands will leave creases.

WRINKLES

Press the ribbon only if needed. Leave the iron upright, set on a medium temperature, and pass the ribbon gently over the plate. Do not press the iron directly on the ribbon; doing so will shrink a silk bias ribbon, crush the pile of a velvet ribbon, and potentially melt a synthetic ribbon.

COLORFASTNESS

A test of colorfastness should be completed on a silk or cotton ribbon if you plan to wash the finished piece. Place a small piece of ribbon in a cup of water for a minute or two. Take the ribbon out and lay it on a white paper towel. If the color bleeds onto the paper towel, you have two options: Rinse the entire length of ribbon or make the design removable so the finished project can be washed without it.

Taking Shape

Transforming the Ribbon

A technique may use a single length of ribbon, or it may use cuts, folds, or loops that are stitched to form the design. Sometimes the width of the ribbon is folded so that the selvage or bias edge becomes an additional detail. Once the ribbon shape is formed, additional thread sculpting or other embellishments may be used to complete the design.

Ribbon Width

Each dimension of a flower, leaf, or garden extra is determined by the width of the ribbon used for the project. The given dimension to cut or measure is described as a multiple of the ribbon width (RW).

Each set of flower directions includes a cutting and measurement chart for that specific design. For the leaves and garden extras, refer to the general chart below for measurements up to 10RW.

Ribbon Cutting Chart*

Ribbon width	Ribbon length								
	2RW	3RW	4RW	5RW	6RW	7RW	8RW	9RW	10RW
1″	2″	3″	4″	5″	6″	7″	8″	9″	10″
⅞″	1¾″	2⅝″	3½″	4⅜″	5¼″	6⅛″	7″	7⅞″	8¾″
¾″	1½″	2¼″	3″	3¾″	4½″	5¼″	6″	6¾″	7½″
⅝″	1¼″	1⅞″	2½″	3⅛″	3¾″	4⅜″	5″	5⅝″	6¼″
½″	1″	1½″	2″	2½″	3″	3½″	4″	4½″	5″
⁷⁄₁₆″	⅞″	1⁵⁄₁₆″	1¾″	2³⁄₁₆″	2⅝″	3¹⁄₁₆″	3½″	3¹⁵⁄₁₆″	4⅜″
⅜″	¾″	1⅛″	1½″	1⅞″	2¼″	2⅝″	3″	3⅜″	3¾″
¼″	½″	¾″	1″	1¼″	1½″	1¾″	2″	2¼″	2½″
⅛″	¼″	⅜″	½″	⅝″	¾″	⅞″	1″	1⅛″	1¼″

Example: When the directions state to measure each petal 3RW, multiply the width of your ribbon 3 times. This will equal the length that you will cut, pin, or fold that dimension. So 3RW of ⅜″ ribbon is 3 × 0.375″ = 1.125″ or 1⅛″.

To find the correct length for a width not included in the Ribbon Cutting Chart, calculate it using the Metric Conversion Chart (page 18) and a calculator.

Measurement Conversion Chart

Inches (⅛″ increments)	Decimal equivalent
1″	1″
¹⁵⁄₁₆″	0.9375″
⅞″	0.875″
¹³⁄₁₆″	0.8125″
¾″	0.75″
¹¹⁄₁₆″	0.6875″
⅝″	0.625″
⁹⁄₁₆″	0.5625″
½″	0.5″
⁷⁄₁₆″	0.4375″
⅜″	0.375″
⁵⁄₁₆″	0.3125″
¼″	0.25″
³⁄₁₆″	0.1875″
⅛″	0.125″
¹⁄₁₆″	0.0625″

In most cases, the widest ribbon used in this book is 1″; you may, of course, use a wider ribbon. The thinnest width listed is ¼″ and in some cases ⅜″, because the narrower the ribbon, the more difficult the technique becomes. If you are feeling adventurous, you can certainly work with any width of ribbon you like.

Ribbon Amounts

Since the length of ribbon required for a ribbonwork project is a factor of the width of the ribbon used, you can expect needed lengths to vary. You will find that the majority of the projects in this book require anywhere from a few inches to a few feet of ribbon, which can be drawn from your ribbon stash. Occasionally, a large flower will require a yard or more of ribbon; in this case I suggest that you check to make sure you have enough ribbon on hand before you start.

To calculate the total amount of ribbon needed for a flower project, refer to the Amount Needed section at the beginning of each project. Simply multiply the width of the ribbon you want to use by the number given to find out the total length of ribbon you will need.

Glossary of Basic Construction Techniques

Ranging from simple to complex, the flowers, leaves, and garden extras are made from either traditional, revamped, or newly devised construction techniques. These techniques include folding, looping, sculpting, or manipulating the ribbon into a variety of shapes. Each design lists suggested ribbons that are suitable for its techniques.

INDIVIDUAL PARTS The ribbon is measured and cut into separate lengths and then folded, knotted, stitched, or looped; the raw edges are then gathered or stitched to a foundation. For a flower, a center might be added to hide the raw edges. The raw edges of a leaf or bud are hidden under a flower.

FLAT LENGTH The length of the ribbon is gathered, with the raw edges angled and tucked behind the middle of the flower to hide them.

Double-Edge Posy, Posy, and Bleeding Heart

Cosmos, Star Lily, and Coneflower

TUBE The raw edges of the ribbon are stitched together to form a circle, and then the inside of the circle is gathered to form the middle of the flower, hiding the raw edges.

Marigold, Ranunculus, and Begonia

BIAS LOOPS The length of ribbon is looped over a piece of cardstock to form the petals and then stitched with a gather stitch (page 26) to create the middle of the flower, hiding the raw edges.

Jasmine, Looped Plume, and Bias-Loop Petals

FOLDED LENGTH The ribbon length is folded in half, and the two edges are stitched as one.

Spanish, Regal, and Arrowhead leaves

FOLDED PETALS OR LOBES The length of ribbon is measured, folded, and pinned to form the sections of the flower or leaf. These are then stitched with a gather stitch (page 26) to create the middle.

Single Peony, Zinnia, and Veronica

SHUTTERBUG PETALS The ribbon is measured and cut into lengths. Each length is then pinned to the next length to form the petals. These are stitched with a gather stitch (page 26) to create the middle of the flower.

Primrose, Vintage Rose, and Persian Violet

RUCHED The length of the ribbon is sewn with a zigzag or ruched stitch (page 26) in sections to create the petals and middle of the flower.

Chrysanthemum, Decorative Dahlia, and Maid's Cap

SINGLE-FOLD PETALS OR LOBES The length of ribbon is measured, folded, and pinned to form two sections of the flower or leaf. It is then stitched with a gather stitch (page 26) to create the middle of the flower or leaf.

Two-Petal Flower, Vine Flower, and Lady's Slipper

SPIRAL   Sections or the entire length of the ribbon are gathered (page 26). One end is stitched to form the center petal, with the remaining length stitched in a spiral around the center.

Lingerie Roses and Victorian Rose

SPIRAL LOOPS   The length of the ribbon is gather stitched (page 26) and then looped over a piece of cardstock to form soft, individual folds. The gathers are pulled in to create the petals and middle of the flower.

Shy Rose, Hollyhock, and Dianthus

U-GATHERS   The length of the ribbon is gathered (page 26) in sections to create the petals and middle of the flower.

Orchid, Gypsy Rose, and U-Gather Petals

Construction Specifics

FLOWERS AND CENTERS

The flowers are made from all of the above techniques; some may also include additional thread sculpting to form the petals. A flower center can be made with a portion of the original length formed into a knot or an additional piece of ribbon tied into a simple knot. A center may also be stitched using one of the above techniques and then attached to the flower.

PETALS AND GREENERY

The techniques you will use for leaf designs are Individual Parts (page 18), Folded Length (page 19), or Folded Petals or Lobes (page 19). These elements, too, may include additional thread sculpting. Several of these designs can be used for either a petal or a leaf; the difference is the color of ribbon you choose to create the design.

GARDEN EXTRAS

The garden extras are made from many of the above techniques with additional ribbon manipulation and thread sculpting. Buds will include stylized versions of a flower design and can also be made from the individual petal or leaf techniques.

You Are the Designer

Country Bonnets, 8″ × 9½″

As you design your ribbonwork arrangements, some artistic license might be necessary and is certainly acceptable when choosing the size, color, and type of ribbons that will work best with the designs you will be using.

Ribbon Auditions

A plain or simple ribbon, such as an inexpensive satin, will work well for a design that requires a lot of ribbon and will look wonderful when used for a complex design. A complex or highly detailed ribbon, such as a jacquard, will make a simple design look elegant.

Each type of ribbon has special qualities that might make it perfect for one technique and not so perfect for another. When choosing the components for your design, match the characteristics of the ribbon to the requirements of the techniques for your chosen components.

Folded- or flat-length designs, such as rosettes and posies, can be made from virtually any type of ribbon. Designs that use bias loops, folded petals, shutterbug petals, two petals, or spiral loops are best suited for a double-sided ribbon with a medium hand. Ruched, U-gather, and spiral techniques are suitable for ribbon with a soft hand.

If you are working with an ombré or variegated ribbon, remember that the side you gather stitch will be the center of the design. If the color changes within the ribbon, note that this may affect the appearance of the design. If a flower calls for the length of the ribbon to be folded for a petal or if the width of the ribbon is folded to create a double edge, use a ribbon that is double-sided. If you are working with a ribbon that is unusually soft or stiff, choose a technique that will work with these qualities.

Flowers made using variegated and ombré ribbons and a picot-edge ribbon

Ribbon Size Choices

Ribbonworked flowers can be round, triangular, or oblong; some will lie flat on the project's surface, while others will have dimension and be raised above the surface. The sample flowers have been stitched using different widths of ribbon to convey the size of one flower compared with that of another. The finished size of the majority of the flower shapes will be twice the width of the ribbon you start with, but some may be smaller or larger depending on the techniques used to create the design.

The leaves can be oblong with a flat or gathered center or folded with a round, square, or pointed tip. For balance, the leaf suggested for a specific flower may be made from the same width of ribbon as the flower or from ribbon that is narrower or wider.

When choosing the width and type of ribbons for your project, keep in mind the finished size and proportion of each of the flowers that you plan to group. An easy formula to start with is a small, a medium, and a large flower. From there you can fill in with additional sizes. When adding leaves, start with the leaf suggested for the largest flower and then fill in with leaves from the smaller flowers.

Blue Jean Baby, 8¼″ × 9″

Flower Details

The design for each flower includes a specific center that may be made from ribbon, a group of millinery stamens, embroidered French knots, seed beads, or a combination.

1. Single Peony   **2.** Cottage Sunflower   **3.** Posy
4. Zinnia   **5.** Sweet Pea   **6.** Lady's Bonnet
7. Double-Edge Rosette   **8.** Aster

Stamens come in a variety of colors, shapes, and sizes and can add a realistic element to the flower. The design may call for a single stamen or a group; these are inserted into the center of the flower and stitched to the wrong side of the ribbon.

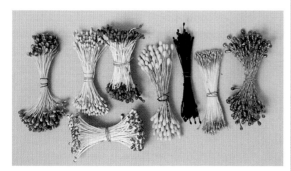

Stamens

Embroidered French knot centers are stitched using a variety of materials including cotton floss, perle cotton, and silk embroidery ribbons. Bead embellishments are stitched using glass beads. French knots can be used in place of beads and vice versa; check the size comparison charts (pages 31 and 32) for suggestions.

If you are stitching the flowers to fabric or gluing them to a mixed-media project, you may want to include a stem or stalk to add a realistic element to your design. A variety of trims can be used for different effects. Rayon rattail cording will make a round stem or stalk that can be curved to form a vine. Satin ribbon or rickrack braid will make a flat stem or stalk, the latter with curved edges.

Rickrack, satin ribbon, and rattail cording

Display Suggestions

The ribbonworked flowers, leaves, and garden extras can be combined with a variety of creative styles and materials to embellish such works as a crazy quilt, an embroidered pillow, a wearable art garment, a mixed-media piece, or any other project you're creating.

For a crazy quilt or fiber-art garment, hand stitch the ribbonwork pieces with a thread that matches the ribbon. For a mixed-media project, attach the ribbonwork with hot glue or tacky glue.

A corsage can be made from a single flower or group of components stitched to a crinoline base, with the back covered by a piece of felt. Or a stem can be made from 22-gauge covered floral wire and glued to the back.

Basic Elements

Velvet Chatelaine, 2¾" × 26", and Pincushion, 1¼"

A Special Note

The teacher in me encourages you to spend a few minutes reading this chapter to familiarize yourself with the technical terms and other concepts covered in the book. The artist in me, however, understands that you want to start creating—and that is okay!

If ribbonwork is new to you, I suggest that you start with the Essential Gardens chapter (page 33) and an inexpensive ribbon, such as satin. This will help you build your body of knowledge and introduce you to many of the techniques that are used in the book.

Skill Levels

The directions for each technique are rated from beginning to advanced skill levels.

SKILL LEVEL: **Easy**

All skill levels

SKILL LEVEL: **Intermediate**

Some practice and experience required

SKILL LEVEL: **Advanced** 🌢🌢🌢

Practice, experience, and skill required

Glossary of Ribbon Edges

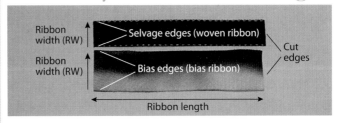

Bias edge Unfinished edge of a bias-cut silk habotai, silk satin, or silk velvet ribbon

Folded edge Edge created when the length or width of the ribbon is folded

Inner edge Edge that will be gathered to create the center of the design

Outer edge Edge that will be farthest from the center of the design

Raw edge Cut ends of ribbon

Ribbon length Measurement between the cut raw edges of ribbon

Ribbon width (RW) Measurement between the selvage or bias edges of ribbon

Selvage edge Finished edge of a woven ribbon

Wire edge Finished edge of a woven ribbon that includes a thin metal wire

Accurate Ribbon Measurement

Place the ribbon on top of a ruler with the newly trimmed raw edge aligned with the exact measurement you need. Fold, cut, loop, or pin the length of ribbon at the end of the ruler.

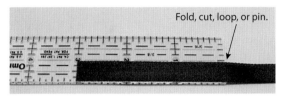
Fold, cut, loop, or pin.

Basic Hand-Sewn Stitches

Once the length is established and the ribbon is cut, folded, looped, or pinned, these sections are then stitched with a variety of stitches to form and hold the shape.

ANCHOR KNOT

An anchor knot is a small knot stitched at the edge of the ribbon. Use this stitch at the beginning of a row of stitches, any time the type of stitch is changed, and to finish a technique.

1. Stitch the needle through the selvage or bias edges of the ribbon.

2. Stitch the needle through the ribbon again; insert the needle through the loop that is created.

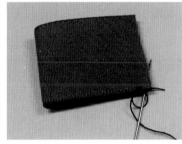

3. Tighten the knot; continue stitching or repeat the knot and cut off the thread.

ASSEMBLY STITCH 1

This is a series of short, even stitches used to stitch two parts of the same ribbon piece together to form a seam, dart, or detail.

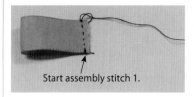
Start assembly stitch 1.

ASSEMBLY STITCH 2

This is a series of short, even stitches used to stitch the raw edges of a seam together.

1. Begin stitching halfway up the seam toward the outer selvage edge.

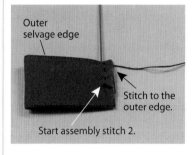
Outer selvage edge
Stitch to the outer edge.
Start assembly stitch 2.

2. Loop the thread over the selvage edge and reverse the stitches back down to the inner selvage edge.

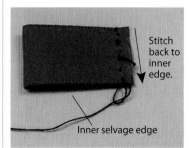
Stitch back to inner edge.
Inner selvage edge

GATHER STITCH

A gather stitch is a series of long, even stitches used to gather the ribbon to form a flower center, a petal, or the bottom edge of a design.

Gather stitch examples

LOOP-OVER

A loop-over stitch wraps over the selvage or bias edge of the ribbon. Use a loop-over each time you change the direction of the gather stitch in order to gather the stitches evenly. It is important that the first stitch after the loop-over maintain the same length as the previous stitches.

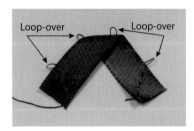

Loop-over examples

TACK STITCH

A tack stitch holds sections of ribbon in place, a flower to a crinoline base, or a center to a flower. Use a stab stitch to tack an area away from the edge of a ribbon. Use a whipstitch to tack an area at the edge of a ribbon.

Stab stitch

Whipstitch

ZIGZAG OR RUCHED STITCH

A zigzag or ruched stitch is a series of long, even gather stitches that are angled toward the selvage edge of a ribbon to form a flower center or a petal.

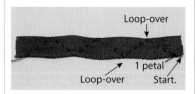

Ruching

Needles and Thread

Milliners needles or sharps, size 10, to stitch ribbon into shape

Beading needles, size 10, to stitch glass beads to ribbon

Chenille needles, sizes 18–24, to embroider using silk embroidery ribbon

Cotton darners, sizes 3–9, to embroider using perle cotton size 5 or 8

Embroidery needles, sizes 3–8, to embroider using three to six strands of cotton, linen, rayon, or silk floss

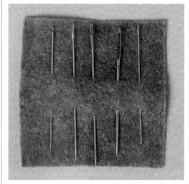

Use a good-quality sewing thread such as Gutermann polyester thread. Keep on hand a wide variety of colors or at least several neutral colors, such as gray, cream, black, red, green, and blue. Use Silamide or Nymo B beading thread to stitch beads and other embellishments onto ribbon.

What's in Your Toolbox?

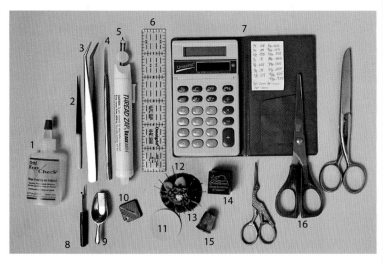

1. **Fray Check** (by Dritz) to keep the raw edges of synthetic or natural-fiber ribbon from fraying

2. **Porcupine quill or plastic stuffing tool** for adding small amounts of stuffing or forming points

3. **Long bent-nose tweezers** for pulling ribbon right side out or tying knots in small lengths of ribbon

4. **Knotting awl or stiletto** to tuck in raw edges

5. **Speedy Wax pen or Thread Zap thread burner,** a battery-powered tool with a heated element to prevent fraying of a synthetic-fiber ribbon by melting the raw edges

6. **Clear quilter's ruler,** 1" × 6", with the measurements marked right to the edge

7. **Calculator** to calculate the ribbon measurements

8. **Seam ripper**

9. **Spoon or scoop** to pick up beads

10. **Needle threader**

11. **Needle gripper or pair of pliers** to pull the needle through layers of ribbon

12. **Thin, sharp appliqué pins**

13. **Pincushion**

14. **Thread Heaven** (by Adam Beadworks) to condition sewing and embroidery threads to minimize knotting

15. **Thimble**

16. **Several pairs of good scissors:** one for woven and silk bias ribbons; one for wire-edge ribbons; one for embroidery thread; and one for paper, crinoline, and cardboard

Also needed (not shown in photo):

Synthetic beeswax to condition beading thread

Good light source, such as an OttLite lamp

Stabilizers

Crinoline is a stiff, loosely woven stabilizer that is available in white and black. Use it as a base for a flower that has individual petals, a flower made from a flat length of gathered ribbon, or a corsage. Buckram can also be used; it is similar to crinoline but with a tighter weave.

To form a crinoline or buckram circle for a project that requires one, draw a square with sides equal to the RW measurement given in the design instructions, usually 2RW. Cut out the square and then mark and trim the corners round.

General Instructions

BEFORE YOU START

■ Carefully read the directions for each design; the techniques vary. The construction techniques of a design may use all or part of the directions from another design; follow these using the ribbon measurements given for your chosen design.

■ Read Basic Hand-Sewn Stitches (page 25) to learn the stitching techniques.

■ Read Types of Ribbon (pages 13–16) for help with choosing the right type and hand of ribbon for a particular design.

■ Read Ribbon Width (page 17) to learn how to measure ribbon.

■ Read Glossary of Basic Construction Techniques (pages 18–20) to master the vocabulary of ribbonwork.

PREPARATION

■ Cut, pin, fold, loop, or knot the ribbon to the exact RW measurement for the design and width of ribbon you are working with.

■ Prepare the ribbon so the raw edges do not fray.

■ Thread the milliners needle or small sharp with 18″ of sewing

thread and knot the tail. (More thread may be needed for longer lengths of ribbon.)

■ If the design calls for a piece of crinoline or cardstock, cut it now.

STITCHING

■ Sew an anchor knot (page 25) into the ribbon. Begin stitching. Anchor knot the thread any time the type of stitch changes, such as from an assembly stitch (page 25) to a gather stitch (page 26).

■ Remove pins after you stitch past them.

■ When gathering a continuous length of ribbon, stop when you get back to the first gather stitch; do not overlap it.

■ Some designs will call for a first thread to gather and a second thread to tack; use the first thread

to adjust the gathers as needed to form the flower.

■ If a design has a crinoline base, trim it so the crinoline does not show beyond the edges of the flower.

FINISHING

Anchor knot the thread two or three times at the end of the stitching. Cut off the excess thread, or leave 6″ of thread to sew the design to a project, as necessary. Add embroidery and beading details as desired, using ideas from Embellishments (pages 30–32).

Pincushion, 2¾″ × 3¾″, and Needle and Thimble Holder, 2½″

Mini Pincushions, 1¾″

Common Questions and Troubleshooting

Silk Petit Four Pincushion, 4″ × 3½″

Why doesn't my flower look like yours?

Honestly, no two flowers of mine ever look quite the same, so don't worry too much! The gathered stitches may not be the same length, the ribbon might have been cut a little longer or shorter than the RW length, or you might have used a different ribbon. Recheck the directions, the suggested type of ribbon, and the RW.

When should I knot and cut the thread?

You may ask why the thread is not always knotted and cut whenever the type of stitch is changed or the stitching moves to a different edge of the ribbon. The techniques are designed to minimize knotting, cutting, and re-knotting the thread because knots can be hard to hide, especially if they start at an outer edge of the ribbon.

What color thread should I use?

Choose a color that matches the ribbon or is slightly darker. In the illustrations I have used a color that will show the stitches clearly.

How do I prevent my thread from knotting?

Cut your sewing or embroidery thread no longer than 18″, and condition it with Thread Heaven to eliminate tangles.

Why is the hole in the center of my flower so big?

The gathered stitches may be too short and too many; longer and fewer stitches will gather the ribbon in to make a smaller hole. Or the ribbon may be too stiff; a velvet ribbon, for instance, will not gather as small as a satin ribbon. Add a larger bead or a button, or stitch a center from ribbon to cover the hole.

How can I prevent frayed edges?

The cut edges of a woven ribbon can fray or unravel as soon as the ribbon is cut. This is certainly annoying, and if you have to trim off the frayed portion of the raw edge, your ribbon can end up too short. To prevent this from happening, either melt or seal the raw edges.

To melt the raw edges of a synthetic woven ribbon, use a Speedy Wax or Thread Zap tool. Run the heat element across the width of each raw edge, or melt the two edges together before they are sewn into a seam. This is an excellent way to fuse the edges of a woven ribbon up to ¼″ wide.

To seal the raw edges of synthetic or natural-fiber ribbon, treat them with Fray Check. Place a small amount of the liquid along each raw edge; or place a small amount along two raw edges held together before they will be sewn into a seam. Try not to let the liquid seep beyond the beginning of the seam because some discoloration may occur. This technique is not recommended for silk bias ribbons, as the liquid will quickly seep beyond the seam.

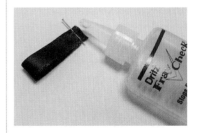

Embellishments

Threads and beads

FRENCH KNOTS

Stitch large French knots, or several small French knots, using silk embroidery ribbon 2mm, 4mm, 7mm, or 13mm wide; perle cotton in sizes 3, 5, 8, or 12; or strands of cotton, rayon, linen, or silk floss. The chart on the next page shows suggested embroidery ribbon or perle cotton sizes or numbers of strands of floss to complement flowers formed from a variety of ribbon widths.

1. Thread the needle and knot the thread tail.

- *For silk embroidery ribbon:* Use a 12"–15" length and a chenille needle.
- *For perle cotton:* Use an 18" length and a cotton darner.
- *For floss:* Use an 18 length and an embroidery needle.

2. Poke the needle up from the wrong side of the flower at the point where you want the knot.

The Details

The directions for a technique may include suggestions for optional details, such as embroidered French knots or glass beads. Use thread or beads in any color that will suit your project and complement the ribbon.

If you are hand stitching the ribbonwork to fabric, you also have the option of adding embellishments before or after you stitch the flower to the fabric. The outer edges of flowers, leaves, and garden extras can also be attached to the fabric with French knots or seed beads. If you are gluing the ribbonwork designs to a project, stitch the embroidered embellishments on first.

The French knots suggested are listed as large, medium, or small and are interchangeable with the beads listed as the same size. Use the charts (pages 31 and 32) as a reference for the width of ribbon and the size of the French knots or beads listed for the design.

3. Hold the needle close to the flower; wrap the thread or ribbon over the needle the number of times suggested in the chart or in the technique directions. Hold the end of the tail of thread with your thumb close to the wraps. Pass the needle down through the flower very close to where it came up; pull the needle through the wrapped knots and to the wrong side of the flower.

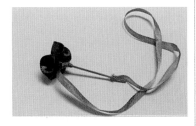

4. Anchor knot and cut the thread after you have finished stitching the French knot or knots.

Rosettes with large French knot or group of small French knots

Size Comparison of French Knots Using Different Threads or Ribbons

Ribbon width used in flower	Large French Knot			Medium French Knot			Small French Knot		
	Number of wraps		Silk embroidery ribbon	Number of wraps		Perle cotton	Number of wraps		Strands of floss
1"		7	13mm		7	Size 3		7	5
⅞"		5	13mm		5	Size 3		5	5
¾"		6	7mm		6	Size 5		6	4
⅝"		4	7mm		4	Size 5		4	4
½"		5	4mm		5	Size 8		5	3
⅜"		3	4mm		4	Size 8		3	3
¼"		4	2mm		4	Size 12		3	2

 tip

Silk Ribbon Embroidery

To knot the ribbon at the beginning:

1. Fold the tail of the ribbon over the needle to create a loop with a fold.

2. Pull the needle out of the loop of ribbon and insert the eye through the fold.

3. Pull the tail out and insert the tip of the needle through the tail.

4. Pull the remaining length of ribbon away from the needle.

This knot will allow you to use all of the ribbon without any waste.

To finish off at the end:

1. Bring the silk ribbon to the back of the work after the final stitch.

2. Weave the ribbon under a few of the stitches on the back.

3. Trim away the excess ribbon.

GLASS BEADS

Glass beads are available in many colors and finishes that can add a nice quality to ribbonwork designs. Large beads (3–8mm) and glass seed beads (sizes 6–15) are used for the beaded details.

Single Bead Center

1. Thread the beading needle with 1 yard of beading thread; double and lightly wax the thread using synthetic beeswax; then knot the tails together.

2. Poke the needle up from the wrong side of the flower at the position where you want the bead. Thread on 1 bead. Stick the needle back into the flower, just beyond the edge of the bead, and through to the wrong side of the flower.

3. Repeat Step 1 to pass the needle through the bead a second time. Anchor knot and cut the thread.

Size Comparison of Glass Beads

Ribbon width used in flower	Large bead	Medium bead	Small bead
1"	8mm	6mm	Size 6
⅞" ¾"	6mm	4mm	Size 8
⅝" ½"	4mm	3mm	Size 11
⅜" ¼"	3mm	Size 6	Size 15

Beaded Edge

1. To attach a finished flower to a display background, thread the beading needle with 1 yard of beading thread. Double and lightly wax the thread using synthetic beeswax; then knot the tails together.

2. Place the flower on the fabric. Poke the needle up from the wrong side, just inside the edge of the flower. Thread on 1 bead. Take the needle to the edge of the bead and pass it through to the wrong side of the flower and fabric.

3. Repeat Step 2, without adding a bead, to stitch through the bead a second time.

4. Repeat Steps 2 and 3 at the place where you want the next bead, and so on, to add more beads. Anchor knot the thread on the wrong side of the fabric after you have finished stitching all of the beads.

Hotflash, 7½" × 7½"

BUTTONS

Shank or sew-through buttons can be stitched into the center of a flower with beading thread or sewing thread.

Stitch the button in place; stitch through the button a second time. Anchor knot and cut the thread.

U-Gather Petals flower with sew-through button and Folded-Edge Posy with shank button

Essential Gardens

The flowers in this chapter use many basic techniques that you may already be familiar with. If you are new to ribbonwork, the flowers here can be used as a stepping-off point for the designs in the chapters that follow.

Most flowers listed in the following chart are accompanied by suggested leaf designs. In some cases, a leaf design is followed by a letter, indicating leaf size:

T = Tiny   **S** = Short   **M** = Medium   **L** = Long   **XL** = Extra-long

For instructions to make the leaves, see Petals and Greenery (page 120).

ROSETTE ... 35
⅜″ taffeta ribbon (striped),
½″ satin ribbon (pink)
Lazy Loop Leaf–T: ⅜″ grosgrain ribbon

DOUBLE-EDGE ROSETTE ... 36
⅝″ silk bias ribbon
Double-Edge Leaf–S: ⅝″ silk bias ribbon

FOLDED-EDGE ROSETTE ... 37
⅝″ silk bias ribbon
Simple Leaf: ⅝″ silk bias ribbon

POSY ... 38
⅜″ grosgrain ribbon (plum),
⅜″ taffeta ribbon (striped)
Pinwheel Leaf: ⅜″ satin ribbon

DOUBLE-EDGE POSY ... 39
⅝″ silk bias ribbon
Kimono Leaf: ⅝″ taffeta ribbon

FOLDED-EDGE POSY ... 40
⅝″ silk bias ribbon
Regal Leaf: ¼″ picot-edged ombré ribbon

FOLDED PETALS ... 41
½″ satin ribbon (mauve),
⅜″ taffeta ribbon (plaid)
Parisian Leaf–S: ⅜″ satin ribbon

TWO-PETAL FLOWER ... 42
⅜″ satin ribbon
Majestic Leaf–M: ⅜″ woven ribbon

U-GATHER PETALS ... 43
⅜″ satin ribbon (pink),
½″ satin ribbon (wine)
Spear-Tip Leaf–M: ⅜″ taffeta ribbon

SHUTTERBUG PETALS ... 44
⅜″ taffeta ribbon
Edwardian Leaf–S: ⅜″ grosgrain ribbon

SPIRAL-LOOP PETALS ... 45
⅜″ grosgrain ribbon
Couture Leaf: ⅜″ satin ribbon

BIAS-LOOP PETALS ... 46
⅜″ satin ribbon
Twin Lazy Loop Leaf–S: ⅜″ double-sided satin ribbon

RUCHED PETALS ... 47
⅜″ satin ribbon
Victorian Leaf–S: ⅜″ double-sided satin ribbon

INDIVIDUAL-PETAL FLOWER ... 48
½″ satin ribbon

Rosette

Rosettes and Lazy Loop Leaf–T (page 122). I suggest using same ribbon width for both flower and leaf.

SKILL LEVEL: *Easy* ⬤

Suggested Ribbon

Woven or French wire ribbon with soft, medium, or stiff hand, single- or double-sided

Amount needed:

■ **Soft-hand ribbon:** 8 × width of project ribbon

■ **Medium-hand ribbon:** 9 × width of project ribbon

■ **Stiff-hand ribbon:** 10 × width of project ribbon

DIRECTIONS

See General Instructions (page 28).

1. Cut 1 length of ribbon (see chart below) according to the hand of the project ribbon. Fold the ribbon length in half, right side in, matching the raw edges. Stitch the raw edges together with a ⅛" seam allowance using assembly stitch 2. Anchor knot the thread into the selvage edges.

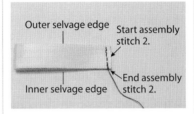

Outer selvage edge — Start assembly stitch 2.
Inner selvage edge — End assembly stitch 2.

2. Starting at the inner selvage edge next to the seam, gather stitch along the continuous selvage edge back to the seam (through only 1 layer of ribbon).

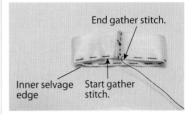

End gather stitch.
Inner selvage edge — Start gather stitch.

3. Gently pull the thread to form the middle of the flower. Anchor knot the thread into the raw edges.

Finished flower. *Detail option:* large French knot (page 30) or bead (page 32)

Measure and Cut

Ribbon width	Soft hand: Cut 1 length 8RW.	Medium hand: Cut 1 length 9RW.	Stiff hand: Cut 1 length 10RW.
1"	8"	9"	10"
⅞"	7"	7⅞"	8¾"
¾"	6"	6¾"	7½"
⅝"	5"	5⅝"	6¼"
½"	4"	4½"	5"
⅜"	3"	3⅜"	3¾"
¼"	2"	2¼"	2½"

Double-Edge Rosette

Double-Edge Rosettes and Double-Edge Leaf–S (page 138). Use same ribbon width for both flower and leaf.

SKILL LEVEL: *Easy* ◗

Suggested Ribbon

Silk bias habotai ribbon

Amount needed:

▪ **Medium-full flower:** 6 × width of project ribbon

▪ **Full flower:** 8 × width of project ribbon

Measure and Cut

Ribbon width	Medium-full flower: Cut 1 length 6RW.	Full flower: Cut 1 length 8RW.
1"	6"	8"
¾"	4½"	6"
⅝"	3¾"	5"
½"	3"	4"
⁷⁄₁₆"	2⅝"	3½"

DIRECTIONS

See General Instructions (page 28).

1. Cut 1 length of ribbon (see chart above) depending on how full you want the flower. Fold and gently finger-press the width of the ribbon to five-eighths the original width.

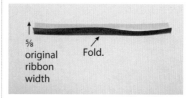

2. Fold the ribbon length in half with the double bias edge inside, matching the raw edges, folded edges, and bias edges. Stitch the raw edges together with a ⅛" seam allowance using assembly stitch 2. Anchor knot the thread into the folded edges.

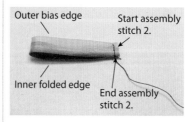

3. Start at the folded edge next to the seam and gather stitch along the continuous folded edge back to the beginning of the seam (through only 1 layer of folded ribbon).

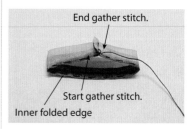

4. Gently pull the thread to form the middle of the flower. Anchor knot the thread into the raw edges.

Finished flower. *Detail option:* Medium bead in center (page 32)

Folded-Edge Rosette

Folded-Edge Rosettes and Simple Leaf (page 125). Use same ribbon width for both flower and leaf.

SKILL LEVEL: *Easy* ◗

Suggested Ribbon

Silk bias ribbon: habotai, satin, or velvet

Amount needed:

■ **Medium-full flower:** 4 × width of project ribbon

■ **Full flower:** 6 × width of project ribbon

Measure and Cut

Ribbon width	Medium-full flower: Cut 1 length 4RW.	Full flower: Cut 1 length 6RW.
1″	4″	6″
¾″	3″	4½″
⅝″	2½″	3¾″
½″	2″	3″
⁷⁄₁₆″	1¾″	2⅝″

DIRECTIONS

See General Instructions (page 28).

1. Cut 1 length of ribbon (see chart above) depending on how full you want the flower. Fold the ribbon length in half, right side in, matching the raw edges. Stitch the raw edges together using assembly stitch 1 and a ⅛″ seam allowance.

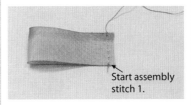
Start assembly stitch 1.

2. Fold and gently finger-press the width of the ribbon in half, right side out. Anchor knot the 2 raw edges together at the seam. Starting next to the seam, gather stitch along 2 continuous bias edges all the way back to the seam (through only 2 bias edges, not all 4).

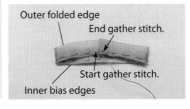
Outer folded edge
End gather stitch.
Start gather stitch.
Inner bias edges

3. Gently pull the thread to form the middle of the flower. Tackstitch through the raw edges and anchor knot the thread.

Finished flower. *Detail option:* 3 small French knots (page 30)

Posy

Posies and Pinwheel Leaf (page 123).
I suggest using same ribbon width for
both flower and leaf.

SKILL LEVEL: *Easy* ⬤

Suggested Ribbon

Woven or French wire ribbon with
soft, medium, or stiff hand, single-
or double-sided

Amount needed:

■ **Soft-hand ribbon:** 8 × width of
project ribbon

■ **Medium-hand ribbon:** 9 × width
of project ribbon

■ **Stiff-hand ribbon:** 10 × width
of project ribbon

DIRECTIONS

See General Instructions (page 28).

1. Cut 1 length of ribbon (see
chart below) according to the
hand of the project ribbon. Insert
a pin 1RW from each raw edge.
Anchor knot the thread into the
outer selvage edge ⅛″ from the
raw edge.

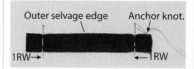

2. Gather stitch at an angle to
the pin at the inner selvage edge;
loop over the edge. Continue
along the selvage edge to the
remaining pin; loop over the edge.
Gather stitch to the outer selvage
edge, ⅛″ from the raw edge.

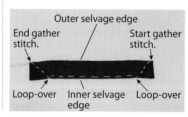

3. Gently pull the thread to form
the middle of the flower. Stitch
through the selvage edge next to
the beginning anchor knot.

4. Match the right sides of
the raw edges. Pull the thread
tight and anchor knot into the
raw edges.

Finished flower. *Detail option:* large bead
in center (page 32)

Measure and Cut

Ribbon width	Soft hand: Cut 1 length 8RW.	Medium hand: Cut 1 length 9RW.	Stiff hand: Cut 1 length 10RW.
1″	8″	9″	10″
⅞″	7″	7⅞″	8¾″
¾″	6″	6¾″	7½″
⅝″	5″	5⅝″	6¼″
½″	4″	4½″	5″
⅜″	3″	3⅜″	3¾″
¼″	2″	2¼″	2½″

Double-Edge Posy

Double-Edge Posies and Kimono Leaf (page 124). Use same ribbon width for both flower and leaf.

SKILL LEVEL: *Easy*

Suggested Ribbon

Silk bias habotai ribbon

Amount needed:

- **Medium-full flower:** 6 × width of project ribbon

- **Full flower:** 8 × width of project ribbon

DIRECTIONS

See General Instructions (page 28).

1. Cut 1 length of ribbon (see chart below) depending on how full you want the flower. Fold and gently finger-press the width of the ribbon to five-eighths the original width. Insert a pin the new folded 1RW measurement from each raw edge.

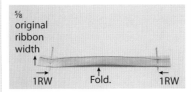

2. Anchor knot the thread into the outer bias edge, ⅛" in from the raw edge. Gather stitch at an angle to the pin at the inner folded edge; loop over the edge. Continue along the folded edge to the remaining pin; loop over the edge. Gather stitch at an angle to the outer bias edge, ⅛" from the raw edge.

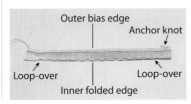

3. Gently pull the thread to form the middle of the flower. Stitch through the bias edges next to the beginning anchor knot.

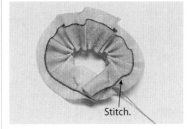

Stitch.

4. Match the right sides of the raw edges. Pull the thread tight and anchor knot into the raw edges.

Finished flower. *Detail option:* large French knot (page 30) or bead (page 32)

Measure and Cut

Ribbon width	Medium-full flower: Cut 1 length 6RW.	Full flower: Cut 1 length 8RW.
1"	6"	8"
¾"	4½"	6"
⅝"	3¾"	5"
½"	3"	4"
⁷⁄₁₆"	2⅝"	3½"

Folded-Edge Posy

Folded-Edge Posies and Regal Leaf (page 135). Use folded width of flower ribbon for leaf ribbon width.

SKILL LEVEL: *Easy* ◗

Suggested Ribbon

Silk bias ribbon: habotai, satin, or velvet

Amount needed:

- **Medium-full flower:** 4 × width of project ribbon

- **Full flower:** 6 × width of project ribbon

DIRECTIONS

See General Instructions (page 28).

1. Cut 1 length of ribbon (see chart below) depending on how full you want the flower. Fold and gently finger-press the width of the ribbon in half. Insert a pin the new folded 1RW measurement from each raw edge.

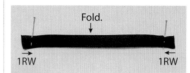

Fold.

1RW   1RW

2. Anchor knot the thread on the outer folded edge ⅛" in from the raw edges. Gather stitch at an angle to the pin at the inner bias edges; loop over the edge. Continue along the bias edges to the remaining pin; loop over the edge. Gather stitch at an angle to the outer folded edge, ⅛" from the raw edges.

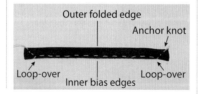

Outer folded edge

Anchor knot

Loop-over   Loop-over
      Inner bias edges

3. Gently pull the thread to form the middle of the flower. Stitch through the folded edge next to the beginning anchor knot.

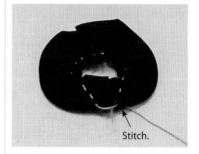

Stitch.

4. Match the right sides of the raw edges. Pull the thread tight and anchor knot into the raw edges.

Finished flower. *Detail option:* medium bead in center (page 32)

Measure and Cut

Ribbon width	Medium-full flower: Cut 1 length 4RW.	Full flower: Cut 1 length 6RW.
1"	4"	6"
¾"	3"	4½"
⅝"	2½"	3¾"
½"	2"	3"
⁷⁄₁₆"	1¾"	2⅝"

Folded Petals

Folded Petals and Parisian Leaf–S (page 123). I suggest using same ribbon width for both flower and leaf.

SKILL LEVEL: *Easy* ◉

Suggested Ribbon

Woven or French wire ribbon with soft or medium hand, double-sided

Amount needed:

■ Approximately 11 × width of project ribbon*

Measure

Ribbon width	Measure 3RW per petal.*
1"	3"
⅞"	2⅝"
¾"	2¼"
⅝"	1⅞"
½"	1½"
⅜"	1⅛"
¼"	¾"

Do not cut the ribbon until instructed to do so.

DIRECTIONS

See General Instructions (page 28).

1. Measure 3RW (see chart below left) in from the raw edge, fold the ribbon down at a 90° angle, and insert a pin through the fold; this is the length of 1 petal. Measure the next 3RW petal from the previous fold; fold the ribbon in the same direction and pin. Measure 3RW from the previous fold and cut off the excess ribbon. Insert a pin 1RW from each raw edge.

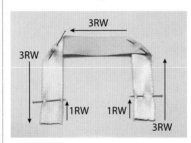

2. Anchor knot the thread on the outer selvage edge ⅛" in from the raw edge. Gather stitch at an angle to the pin at the inner selvage edge; loop over the edge. Continue along each selvage edge and through each fold to the last pin; loop over each edge. Gather stitch at an angle to the outer selvage edge, ⅛" from the raw edge.

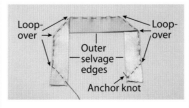

3. Gently pull the thread to form the petals. Stitch through the selvage edge next to the beginning anchor knot.

4. Match the right sides of the raw edges. Pull the thread tight and anchor knot into the raw edges.

Finished flower. *Detail option:* large French knot (page 30) or bead (page 32)

Two-Petal Flower

Two-Petal Flower and Majestic Leaf–M (page 131). Use same ribbon width for both flower and leaf.

SKILL LEVEL: *Easy* 💧

Suggested Ribbon

Woven or French wire ribbon with soft or medium hand, double-sided

Amount needed:

- Approximately 9 × width of project ribbon*

Measure

Ribbon width	Measure 4RW per petal.*
1″	4″
⅞″	3½″
¾″	3″
⅝″	2½″
½″	2″
⅜″	1½″
¼″	1″

* Do not cut the ribbon until instructed to do so.

DIRECTIONS

See General Instructions (page 28).

1. Measure 4RW (see chart below left) in from the raw edge, fold the ribbon down at a 90° angle, and insert a pin through the fold. Measure 4RW from the fold and cut off the excess ribbon. Insert a pin 1RW from each raw edge.

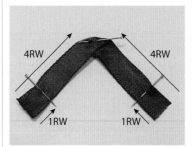

2. Anchor knot the thread on the outer selvage edge ⅛″ in from the raw edge. Gather stitch at an angle toward the inner selvage edge to the first pin; loop over the edge. Continue along the selvage edge, through the fold and the next selvage edge to the last pin; loop over each edge. Gather stitch at an angle to the outer selvage edge, ⅛″ from the raw edge.

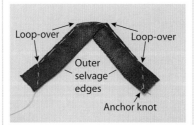

3. Gently pull the thread to form the petals. Stitch through the selvage edge next to the beginning anchor knot.

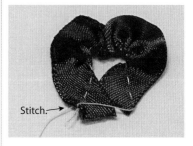

4. Match the right sides of the raw edges. Pull the thread tight and anchor knot into the raw edges.

Finished flower

U-Gather Petals

U-Gather Petals and Spear-Tip Leaf–M (page 126). I suggest using same ribbon width for both flower and leaf.

SKILL LEVEL: *Easy* ◐

Suggested Ribbon

Woven ribbon with soft or medium hand, single- or double-sided

Amount needed:

■ Approximately 16 × width of project ribbon, plus ½" *

Measure

Ribbon width	Measure 4RW per petal.*
1"	4"
⅞"	3½"
¾"	3"
⅝"	2½"
½"	2"
⅜"	1½"
¼"	1"

* Do not cut the ribbon until instructed to do so.

DIRECTIONS

See General Instructions (page 28).

1. Insert a pin ¼" in from the raw edge. Measure 4RW (see chart below left) from the pin and insert another pin; this is the length of 1 petal. Measure each of the next 3 petals from the pin of the previous petal. Cut the ribbon ¼" beyond the last pin.

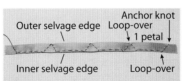

2. Anchor knot the thread at the first pin and outer selvage edge.

3. Gather stitch at an angle ¼" away from the pin to the inner selvage edge; loop over the edge. Continue along the selvage edge, stopping ¼" before the next pin; loop over the edge. Gather stitch at an angle toward the pin at the outer selvage edge; loop over the edge. This completes 1 petal. Repeat for each of the remaining 3 petals.

4. Gently pull the thread to form the middle of the flower. Stitch through the selvage edge next to the beginning anchor knot.

5. Match the right sides of the raw edges. Pull the thread tight and anchor knot into the raw edges.

Finished flower. Small V-shaped sections form inner petals.

Shutterbug Petals

Shutterbug Petals and Edwardian Leaf–S (page 129). Use same ribbon width for both flower and leaf.

SKILL LEVEL: *Easy* ◗

Suggested Ribbon

Woven ribbon with soft or medium hand, single- or double-sided

Amount needed:

- 16 × width of project ribbon

Measure and Cut

Ribbon width	Cut 4 lengths 4RW.
1"	4"
⅞"	3½"
¾"	3"
⅝"	2½"
½"	2"
⅜"	1½"
¼"	1"

DIRECTIONS

See General Instructions (page 28).

1. Cut 4 lengths of ribbon 4RW (see chart below left). Overlap and align the raw edge of the first length with the selvage edge of the next length, right sides up. Insert a pin through both layers. This forms the first petal. Repeat for each remaining petal, overlapping the last petal over the first.

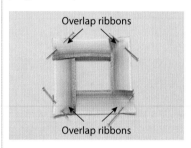

2. Anchor knot the thread into the top right corner section, 1RW down from the top petal's outer selvage edge. Gather stitch diagonally through both layers of ribbon across the corner section toward the opposite selvage edge; loop over the edge. Gather stitch along all the outer selvage edges and diagonally across the corner sections, looping over each edge, all the way back to the beginning anchor knot.

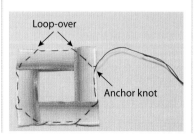

3. Gently pull the thread to form the petals and the middle of the flower. Push the raw edges into the opening and to the wrong side of the flower; pull the thread tight. Tackstitch through the raw edges and anchor knot the thread.

Finished flower. *Detail option:* medium French knot (page 30) or bead (page 32)

Spiral-Loop Petals

Spiral-Loop Petals and Couture Leaf (page 122). Use same ribbon width for flower and leaf.

SKILL LEVEL: *Intermediate* ◗◗

Suggested Ribbon

Woven ribbon with soft or medium hand, single- or double-sided

Amount needed:

- 12 × width of project ribbon

Additional Supplies

- 1RW × 8″ strip of cardstock

Measure and Cut

Ribbon width	Cut 1 length 12RW.
1″	12″
⅞″	10½″
¾″	9″
⅝″	7½″
½″	6″
⅜″	4½″
¼″	3″

DIRECTIONS

See General Instructions (page 28).

1. Cut 1 length of ribbon 12RW (see chart below left). Insert a pin 1RW from each raw edge. Anchor knot the thread where the first pin meets the inner selvage edge. Gather stitch along the inner selvage edge to the last pin; keep the needle threaded, and do not anchor or cut the thread.

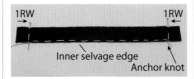

2. Evenly loop the ribbon 3 times over the cardstock; the heads of the pins should be facing the same direction.

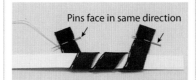

3. Match the raw edges. Gather stitch through both layers of ribbon diagonally toward the point on the outer selvage edge that is ⅛″ from the raw edge. Remove the cardstock.

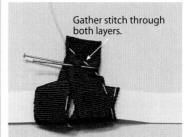

Sample has been flipped to reveal stitching on underside.

4. Gently pull the thread to form the petals of the flower; the raw edges will curve up. Anchor knot the thread into the raw edges.

Finished flower

Bias-Loop Petals

Bias-Loop Petals with Twin Lazy Loop Leaf–S (page 134). Use same ribbon width for both flower and leaf.

SKILL LEVEL: *Intermediate*

Suggested Ribbon

Woven ribbon with medium hand, double-sided

Amount needed:

- Approximately 18½ × width of project ribbon*

Additional Supplies

- 1RW × 8″ strip of cardstock

Measure

Ribbon width	Measure 18½RW.*
1″	18½″
⅞″	16³⁄₁₆″
¾″	13⅞″
⅝″	11⁹⁄₁₆″
½″	9¼″
⅜″	6¹⁵⁄₁₆″
¼″	4⅝″

* Do not cut the ribbon until instructed to do so.

DIRECTIONS

See General Instructions (page 28).

1. Insert a pin 1RW in from a raw edge. Fold the ribbon at an angle over the cardstock, with the pin at the edge of the cardstock. Remove the pin and reinsert through the first petal and the cardstock.

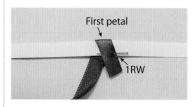

2. Loosely wrap and fold 5 more petals. Measure 1RW, cut off the excess ribbon, and insert a pin through the last petal and the cardstock.

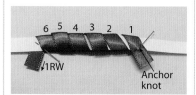

3. Anchor knot the thread at the beginning selvage edge of the first petal. Using the edge of the cardstock as a guide, gather stitch across the width of the first raw edge, the folds, and the last raw edge. Unpin and remove the cardstock.

4. Stitch through the selvage edge next to the beginning anchor knot.

5. Gently pull the thread to form the middle of the flower and tackstitch through the raw edges. Anchor knot the thread into the raw edges.

Finished flower

Ruched Petals

Ruched Petals and Victorian Leaf–S (page 130). Use same ribbon width for both flower and leaf.

SKILL LEVEL: *Intermediate* 🌑🌑

Suggested Ribbon

Woven ribbon with soft or medium hand, single- or double-sided

Amount needed:

▪ Approximately 12 × width of project ribbon, plus ½" *

Measure

Ribbon width	Measure 2RW per petal.*
1"	2"
⅞"	1¾"
¾"	1½"
⅝"	1¼"
½"	1"
⅜"	¾"

* Do not cut the ribbon until instructed to do so.

DIRECTIONS

See General Instructions (page 28).

1. Insert a pin ¼" from the raw edge. Measure 2RW (see chart below left) and insert a pin; this is the length of 1 petal. Measure each of the remaining 5 petals from the last pin of the previous petal. Measure ¼" from the last petal and cut off the excess ribbon.

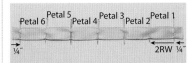

2. Fold the length of the ribbon in half between the first and second pin and crease to mark the fold. Anchor knot the thread where the first pin meets the outer selvage edge.

3. Gather stitch at an angle toward the crease at the inner selvage edge; loop over the edge. Reverse direction and gather stitch at an angle to the next pin at the outer selvage edge; loop over the edge. This completes 1 petal. For the next petal, fold the length of ribbon in half between the next 2 pins and crease to mark the fold. Repeat for each of the remaining 5 petals.

The selvage edge facing you as you stitch is the outer edge of the flower; the outer edge has 1 more petal than the inner edge.

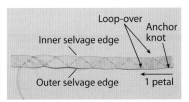

4. Gently pull the thread to form the middle of the flower. Stitch through the selvage edge next to the beginning anchor knot.

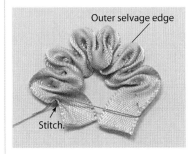

5. Match the right sides of the raw edges. Pull the thread tight and anchor knot into the raw edges.

Finished flower

Individual-Petal Flower

Lazy Loop Petal flower (page 122). Combine finished flower with leaf of your choice.

SKILL LEVEL: *Intermediate* 🌢🌢

Any of the individual petal designs in Petals and Greenery (page 120) can be used to create a flower.

DIRECTIONS

See General Instructions (page 28).

1. Follow the suggested ribbon and RW length given for the petal design. Cut 5 lengths of ribbon; work with 1 length at a time. Follow the pin, fold, or stitch directions for the petal design. (The number of petals can be increased or decreased.) Arrange the petals side by side, ready for stitching.

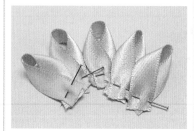

2. Anchor knot the thread into the selvage edge ⅛" from the raw edge of the first petal. Gather stitch across the petals, ⅛" from the raw edges. The gather stitching may cause the petals to overlap slightly as you work.

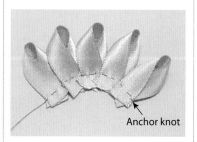

Anchor knot

3. Gently pull the thread to form the middle of the flower. Stitch through the selvage edge next to the beginning anchor knot.

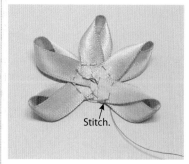

Stitch.

4. Push the raw edges into the opening and to the wrong side of the flower; pull the thread tight. Tackstitch through the raw edges and anchor knot the thread.

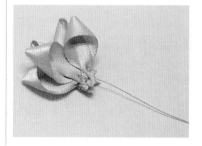

Finished flower

Cottage Gardens

These flowers are reminiscent of white picket fences, charming gardens full of wind chimes, and bees buzzing busily among the garden's treasures. They are a sweet reminder of summer days spent lazily swinging on a hammock or tire swing enjoying the innocent floral fragrance with a glass of homemade lemonade.

SINGLE PEONY ... 51
⅜″ satin ribbon
Crown Leaf: ⅜″ satin ribbon

DAFFODIL ... 52
⅜″ satin ribbon
Regal Leaf: ¼″ picot-edged ombré ribbon

VIOLA ... 53
⅜″ satin ribbon
Edwardian Leaf–M: ⅜″ satin ribbon

TRILLIUM ... 54
½″ satin ribbon
Spanish Leaf–M: ⅜″ woven ombré ribbon

DELPHINIUM ... 55
⅝″ grosgrain ribbon
Fleur-de-Lis Leaf: ⅝″ grosgrain ribbon

GILLYFLOWER ... 56
⅜″ satin ribbon
Lazy Loop Leaf–S: ⅜″ velvet ribbon

LADY'S BONNET ... 57
⅜″ grosgrain and ¼″ ombré picot-edged ribbons
Jester's Leaf: ⅜″ grosgrain ribbon

MARIGOLD ... 58
⅝″ silk bias ribbon
Edwardian Leaf–M: ⅜″ satin ribbon

SNAPDRAGON ... 59
⅜″ satin ribbon
Teardrop Leaf–S: ⅜″ satin ribbon

LADY'S SLIPPER ... 60
⅜″ satin ribbon
Victorian Leaf–S: ⅜″ satin ribbon

TRIPLE DELIGHT ... 61
⅝″ silk bias ribbon
Rounded Leaf–M: 1″ silk bias ribbon

DANDELION ... 62
¼″ satin ribbon

COTTAGE SUNFLOWER ... 63
⅝″ satin and ¼″ woven ribbons
Victorian Leaf–L: ⅝″ satin ribbon

Single Peony

Single Peony and Crown Leaf (page 133). Use same ribbon width for both flower and leaf.

SKILL LEVEL: *Intermediate* ◖◗

Suggested Ribbon

Woven or French wire ribbon with soft or medium hand, double-sided

Amount needed:

▪ Approximately 24 × width of project ribbon*

Additional Supplies

▪ 2RW crinoline circle

▪ Second threaded needle

▪ 3 folded stamens

Measure

Ribbon width	Measure 4RW per petal.*
1"	4"
⅞"	3½"
¾"	3"
⅝"	2½"
½"	2"
⅜"	1½"

* Do not cut the ribbon until instructed to do so.

DIRECTIONS

See General Instructions (page 28) and Folded Petals (page 41).

1. Measure, pin, and gather stitch 5 folded petals 4RW each (see chart below left). Gently pull the thread to form the petals; keep the needle threaded, and do not anchor or cut the thread.

2. At the beginning anchor knot, use the second needle to tackstitch the ribbon to the crinoline.

3. Poke a small hole in the center of the crinoline and insert the stamens through the opening. Place the beginning raw edge of the ribbon over the opening and tackstitch in place.

4. Tackstitch the first petal over the raw edges. Tackstitch the second petal opposite the first petal.

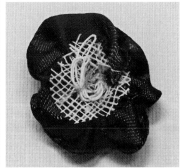

5. Tackstitch the 3 remaining petals around and under the center petals. Trim the crinoline. Tackstitch the raw edges of the last petal to the back of the crinoline. Anchor knot both threads to the crinoline.

Finished flower

Daffodil

Daffodil and Regal Leaf (page 135). Use ribbon ⅛" narrower for leaf than for flower.

SKILL LEVEL: *Intermediate* ◖◖

Suggested Ribbon

2 different colors of woven ribbon with soft or medium hand, single- or double-sided

Amount needed:

- **Flower:** Approximately 18 × width of Color 1 ribbon, plus ½" *
- **Center:** 4 × width of Color 2 ribbon

Measure and Cut

Ribbon width	Flower: Measure 3RW per petal.*	Center: Cut 1 length 4RW.
1"	3"	4"
⅞"	2⅝"	3½"
¾"	2¼"	3"
⅝"	1⅞"	2½"
½"	1½"	2"
⅜"	1⅛"	1½"

* Do not cut the ribbon until instructed below.

DIRECTIONS

See General Instructions (page 28), Ruched Petals (page 47), and Rosette (page 35).

1. Flower: Measure, pin, and stitch a six-petal ruched petal flower with 3RW petals (see chart above), and cut the thread.

2. Center: Cut 1 length of ribbon 4RW (see chart above). Make a rosette. The short length will form a cup; do not cut the thread.

3. Tackstitch the center into the middle petals of the flower through the seam of the center. Anchor knot the thread into the raw edges of the flower.

Finished flower

Viola

Viola and Edwardian Leaf–M (page 129). Use same ribbon width for both flower and leaf.

SKILL LEVEL: *Intermediate* ◖◖

Suggested Ribbon

2 different colors of woven or French wire ribbon with medium hand, double-sided

Amount needed:

- **Lower petals:** Approximately 11 × width of Color 1 ribbon*

- **Upper petals:** Approximately 9 × width of Color 2 ribbon*

Additional Supplies

- Silk embroidery ribbon

DIRECTIONS

See General Instructions (page 28), Folded Petals (page 41), and Two-Petal Flower (page 42).

1. Lower petals: Measure and pin a three-petal folded petal flower with 3RW petals (see chart below) with the folds facing inward.

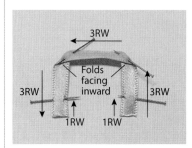

2. Follow the gather-stitch and assembly stitch directions; cut off the thread.

3. Upper petals: Measure and pin a two-petal flower 4RW (see chart below left). Follow the gather-stitch directions and gently pull the thread to form the petals; do not cut the thread.

4. Tackstitch the raw edges of the upper petals into the raw edges of the lower petals and anchor knot the thread. Stitch a large French knot (page 30) for the center.

Finished flower

Measure

Ribbon width	Lower petals: Measure 3RW per petal.*	Upper petals: Measure 4RW per petal.*
1"	3"	4"
⅞"	2⅝"	3½"
¾"	2¼"	3"
⅝"	1⅞"	2½"
½"	1½"	2"
⅜"	1⅛"	1½"
¼"	¾"	1"

* Do not cut the ribbon until instructed to do so.

Trillium

Trillium and Spanish Leaf–M (page 128). Use ribbon ⅛" narrower for leaf than for flower.

SKILL LEVEL: *Intermediate* ◗ ◗

Suggested Ribbon

Woven or French wire ribbon with soft or medium hand, single- or double-sided

Amount needed:

- 9 × width of project ribbon

Additional Supplies

- 2 folded stamens

Measure and Cut

Ribbon width	Cut 3 lengths 3RW.
1"	3"
⅞"	2⅝"
¾"	2¼"
⅝"	1⅞"
½"	1½"
⅜"	1⅛"

DIRECTIONS

See General Instructions (page 28).

1. Petals: Cut 3 lengths of ribbon 3RW (see chart below left). Fold the first ribbon length in half; anchor knot the thread into the inner selvage edges ½RW from the fold. Using assembly stitch 1, stitch diagonally to the tip of the fold; stitch back to the inner selvage edges. Anchor knot and cut the thread. Repeat for each petal; open each petal flat.

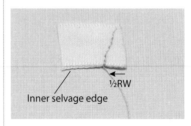

½RW

Inner selvage edge

2. Flower: Overlap the left half of the first petal over the right half of the second petal. Align the corners and insert pins through both layers. Repeat for the second and third petals. Anchor knot the thread into the selvage edge at the seam of the first petal. Gather stitch across the petals between the seams, through both layers of ribbon.

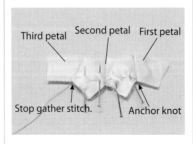

Third petal   Second petal   First petal

Stop gather stitch.   Anchor knot

3. Overlap the left half of the third petal over the right half of the first petal and insert a pin through both layers. Working from the wrong side, gather stitch across the remaining petals.

Continue gather stitch to here.

4. Gently pull the thread to form the middle of the flower. Insert the stamens through the opening of the flower; pull the thread tight to close the opening. Tackstitch through the raw edges and anchor knot the thread.

Finished flower

Delphinium

Delphinium and Fleur-de-Lis Leaf (page 127). Use same ribbon width for flower and leaf.

SKILL LEVEL: *Advanced* ●●●

Suggested Ribbon

Woven ribbon with soft or medium hand, double-sided

Amount needed:

■ **Center:** 9 × width of project ribbon

■ **Flower:** Approximately 27 × width of project ribbon, plus ½" *

DIRECTIONS

See General Instructions (page 28), Shutterbug Center (page 144), and Ruched Petals (page 47).

1. Center: Cut 3 lengths of ribbon 3RW (see chart below). Follow the directions to make a shutterbug center; cut the thread. The petals will curve in.

2. Flower: Measure, pin, and gather stitch 9 ruched petals 3RW (see chart below). Gently pull the thread to form the middle of the flower. Stitch through the selvage edge next to the beginning anchor knot.

Stitch.

3. Insert the raw edge of the center into the middle of the flower and pull the thread tight to close the flower petals around the center. Arrange the inner petals around the outer sides of the center. Tackstitch through the gather stitches of the flower to the raw edges of the center. Anchor knot the thread into the raw edges.

Finished flower. *Detail option:* 5 medium French knots (page 30) or beads (page 32)

Measure and Cut

Ribbon width	Center: Cut 3 lengths 3RW.	Flower: Measure 3RW per petal.*
1"	3"	3"
⅞"	2⅝"	2⅝"
¾"	2¼"	2¼"
⅝"	1⅞"	1⅞"
½"	1½"	1½"
⅜"	1⅛"	1⅛"

* Do not cut the ribbon until instructed to do so.

Gillyflower

Gillyflower and Lazy Loop Leaf–S (page 122). Use same ribbon width for both flower and leaf.

SKILL LEVEL: **Easy** 🌢

Suggested Ribbon

2 different colors of woven ribbon with soft or medium hand, double-sided

Amount needed:

■ **Center petals:** 9 × width of Color 1 ribbon

■ **Outer petals:** 18 × width of Color 2 ribbon

Measure and Cut

Ribbon width	Center petals: Cut 3 lengths 3RW.	Outer petals: Cut 3 lengths 6RW.
1″	3″	6″
⅞″	2⅝″	5¼″
¾″	2¼″	4½″
⅝″	1⅞″	3¾″
½″	1½″	3″
⅜″	1⅛″	2¼″

DIRECTIONS

See General Instructions (page 28) and Shutterbug Center (page 144).

1. Center petals: Cut 3 lengths of ribbon 3RW (see chart above). Follow the directions to make a shutterbug center; cut the thread. The petals will curve in.

2. Outer petals: Cut 3 lengths of ribbon 6RW (see chart above). Follow the pinning and gather-stitch directions for the shutterbug center.

3. Insert the raw edges of the center into the opening of the outer petals and pull the thread tight to close the middle. Tackstitch through the raw edges and anchor knot the thread.

Finished flower. *Detail option*: large French knot (page 30) or bead (page 32)

Lady's Bonnet

Lady's Bonnet and Jester's Leaf (page 130). Use same ribbon width for both flower and leaf.

SKILL LEVEL: **Easy** ◊

Suggested Ribbon

2 different widths and colors of woven ribbon with soft or medium hand, single- or double-sided

Amount needed:

■ **Color 1:** 14 × width of wider ribbon

■ **Color 2:** 14 × width of wider ribbon (Use ⅛" narrower ribbon for Color 2, cut the same length as Color 1.)

Measure and Cut

Width of wider ribbon	Bottom petal: Cut 1 length of each color.	Top petal: Cut 1 length of each color.
1"	8"	6"
⅞"	7"	5¼"
¾"	6"	4½"
⅝"	5"	3¾"
½"	4"	3"
⅜"	3"	2¼"
¼"	2"	1½"

DIRECTIONS

See General Instructions (page 28), Layering Ribbon (page 16), Posy (page 38), and Fan (page 140).

1. Bottom petal: Cut 1 length of ribbon of each color (see chart above). Follow the directions for layering and for making a posy, and cut the thread.

2. Top petal: Cut 1 length of ribbon from each color (see chart above). Follow the directions for layering and for making a fan all the way through pulling the gather stitches, but do not cut the thread.

3. Place the top petal under the bottom petal. Tackstitch the raw edges of the top petal into the raw edges of the bottom petal. Anchor knot the thread.

Finished flower. *Detail option*: small button (page 32)

Marigold

Marigold and Edwardian Leaf–M (page 129). Use folded ribbon width of flower for leaf ribbon width.

SKILL LEVEL: *Easy* ◖

Suggested Ribbon

2 different colors of silk bias habotai ribbon

Amount needed:

- **Inner layer:** 12 × width of Color 1 ribbon

- **Outer layer:** 16 × width of Color 2 ribbon

Additional Supplies

- 2RW crinoline circle

Measure and Cut

Ribbon width	Inner layer: Cut 1 length 12RW.	Outer layer: Cut 1 length 16RW.
1″	12″	16″
¾″	9″	12″
⅝″	7½″	10″
½″	6″	8″
⁷⁄₁₆″	5¼″	7″

DIRECTIONS

See General Instructions (page 28) and Double-Edge Rosette (page 36).

1. Inner layer: Cut 1 length of ribbon 12RW (see chart below). Make a double-edge rosette but do not cut the thread. Stitch into the center of the crinoline.

2. Tackstitch the middle of the inner layer to the crinoline; anchor knot and cut the thread.

3. Outer layer: Cut 1 length of ribbon 16RW (see chart below left). Follow the directions for a double-edge rosette through the gather stitching. Gently pull the thread to gather the outer layer.

4. Arrange the outer layer under the inner layer, on top of the crinoline. Gently pull the thread to close the opening of the outer layer. Tackstitch the inner gathers to the crinoline and anchor knot the thread.

Finished flower

Snapdragon

Snapdragon and Teardrop Leaf–S (page 129). Use same ribbon width for flower and leaf.

SKILL LEVEL: *Intermediate* 🌢🌢

Suggested Ribbon

Woven or French wire ribbon with soft or medium hand, single- or double-sided

Amount needed:

- 14 × width of project ribbon

Measure and Cut

Ribbon width	Cut 1 length 14RW.
1″	14″
⅞″	12¼″
¾″	10½″
⅝″	8¾″
½″	7″
⅜″	5¼″

DIRECTIONS

See General Instructions (page 28).

1. Cut 1 length of ribbon 14RW (see chart below left).

Center: Fold the ribbon length in half, right side in. Anchor knot the thread into the selvage edges 3RW from the fold. Gather stitch at a slightly curved angle toward the opposite corner of the fold.

2. Gently pull the thread to form the center. Tackstitch back through the gathers to the beginning selvage edges. Anchor knot, but do not cut the thread.

3. Outer petals: Insert a pin 1RW from each raw edge.

4. For the first petal, gather stitch along the inner selvage edge to the pin; loop over the edge. Gather stitch diagonally toward the point on the opposite selvage that is ⅛″ from the raw edge.

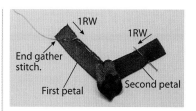

5. Gently pull the thread to form the petal.

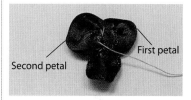

6. Tackstitch into the raw edges and anchor knot the thread. Repeat Steps 4–6 for the second petal, overlapping the second petal behind the first petal.

Finished flower

Lady's Slipper

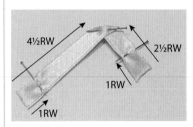

Lady's Slipper and Victorian Leaf–S (page 130). Use same ribbon width for flower and leaf.

SKILL LEVEL: *Easy* 🌿

Suggested Ribbon

Woven or French wire with soft or medium hand, double-sided

Amount needed:

■ Approximately 8 × width of ribbon*

DIRECTIONS

See General Instructions (page 28) and Two-Petal Flower (page 42).

1. Upper petal: Measure 2½RW (see chart below) from the raw edge; fold the ribbon down at a 90° angle; insert a pin through the fold.

Lower petal: Measure 4½RW (see chart below) from the fold; cut off the excess ribbon. Insert a pin 1RW from each raw edge.

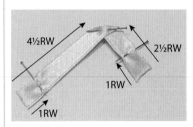

2. Follow the gather-stitch directions for the two-petal flower.

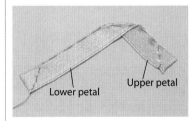

3. Gently pull the thread to form the 2 petals of the flower.

4. Match the right sides of the raw edges. Overlap the upper petal over the lower petal; pull the thread tight. Tackstitch and anchor knot into the raw edges.

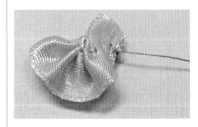

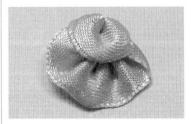

Finished flower

Measure

Ribbon width	Upper petal: Measure 2½RW per petal.*	Lower petal: Measure 4½RW per petal.*
1"	2½"	4½"
⅞"	2³⁄₁₆"	3¹⁵⁄₁₆"
¾"	1⅞"	3⅜"
⅝"	1⁹⁄₁₆"	2¹³⁄₁₆"
½"	1¼"	2¼"
⅜"	¹⁵⁄₁₆"	1¹¹⁄₁₆"
¼"	⅝"	1⅛"

* Do not cut the ribbon until instructed to do so.

Triple Delight

Triple Delight and Rounded Leaf–M (page 137). Use ribbon ⅜″ wider for leaf than for flower.

SKILL LEVEL: *Intermediate* ●●

Suggested Ribbon

Silk bias habotai ribbon

Amount needed:

■ Approximately 9 × width of flower ribbon, plus ½″ *

Measure

Ribbon width	Measure 3RW per petal.*
1″	3″
¾″	2¼″
⅝″	1⅞″
½″	1½″
⁷⁄₁₆″	1⁵⁄₁₆″

* Do not cut the ribbon until instructed to do so.

DIRECTIONS

See General Instructions (page 28) and U-Gather Petals (page 43).

1. Fold and gently finger-press the width of the ribbon to five-eighths the original width. Measure and pin 3 U-gather petals 3RW each (see chart below left).

First petal: Follow the gather-stitch directions to make a U-gather petal.

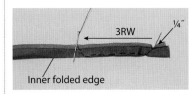

2. Loop the thread over the entire width of the ribbon; stitch through the folded edge next to the beginning anchor knot. Pull the thread tight and anchor knot it.

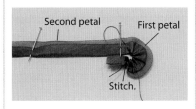

3. Second petal: Beginning at the fold, gather stitch to make a U-gather petal; repeat Step 2 for this petal.

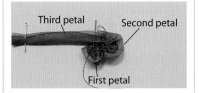

4. Third petal: Begin again at the fold and gather stitch to make another U-gather petal.

5. Gently pull the thread; tack-stitch the raw edges to the wrong side of the flower. Anchor knot the thread.

Finished flower. *Detail option*: 3 small French knots (page 30) or beads (page 32)

Dandelion

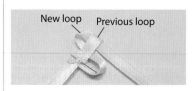

Dandelion

SKILL LEVEL: *Intermediate* 🔹🔹

Suggested Ribbon

Woven ribbon with soft, medium, or stiff hand, double-sided

Amount needed:

- 144 × width of project ribbon

DIRECTIONS

See General Instructions (page 28).

1. Cut 1 length of ribbon 144RW (see chart above right). Fold the length in half; insert a pin through the fold. Fold a small loop, with the free side facing up.

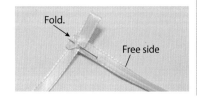

2. Fold the free side behind the loop.

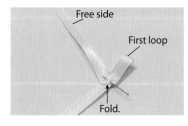

Measure and Cut

Ribbon width	Cut 1 length 144 RW.
¾"	108"
⅝"	90"
½"	72"
⅜"	54"
¼"	36"
⅛"	18"

3. Fold the length into a loop; insert the new loop through the previous loop.

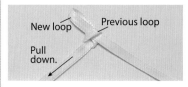

4. Pull the length of ribbon connected to the first loop down.

5. Beginning with the length of ribbon connected to the first loop, repeat Steps 3 and 4, alternating between lengths, down the entire length of both halves of the ribbon.

6. Insert the tail of the ribbon without a loop.

7. Fold the remaining length under the tail and place a pin through both layers of ribbon.

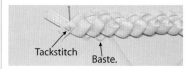

8. Tackstitch the 2 ribbon halves together. Stitch a long basting stitch into the middle of each loop along one side.

9. Gently pull the thread to form the middle of the center. Stitch through the selvage edge next to the beginning anchor knot.

10. Overlap the beginning end over the raw edges of the last fold. Tackstitch both sides in place. Cut off any excess ribbon and anchor knot the thread into the raw edges.

Finished flower

Cottage Sunflower

Cottage Sunflower and Victorian Leaf–L (page 130). Use same ribbon width for petals and leaf.

SKILL LEVEL: *Intermediate* 🌢🌢

Suggested Ribbon

2 different widths and colors of woven or French wire ribbon with soft or medium hand, single- or double-sided

Amount needed:

- **Center:** 144 × width of Color 1 ribbon (Use a ⅜" narrower ribbon than for petals.)

- **Petals:** 36 × width of Color 2 ribbon

Additional Supplies

- 1 crinoline circle slightly smaller than the finished center

Measure and Cut

Center		Petals	
Ribbon width	Cut 1 length 144RW.	Ribbon width	Cut 12 lengths 3RW.
¾"	108"	1⅛"	3⅜"
⅝"	90"	1"	3"
½"	72"	⅞"	2⅝"
⅜"	54"	¾"	2¼"
¼"	36"	⅝"	1⅞"
⅛"	18"	½"	1½"

DIRECTIONS

See General Instructions (page 28); Dandelion (page 62); and Kimono Leaf, Petal, or Bud (page 124).

1. Center: Cut a length of ribbon 144RW (see chart above). Follow the directions for the dandelion; cut off the excess thread.

2. Petals: Cut 12 lengths of ribbon 3RW (see chart above). Follow the directions to make a kimono petal from each length, folding the left side over the right. Cut the threads.

3. Stitch through the raw edge of each petal at the gathered seam. Stitch back through the first petal to form a ring.

4. Gently pull the thread to close the ring ¼" smaller than the crinoline. Tackstitch the raw edges of each petal to the crinoline.

5. Arrange the center on top of the raw edges of the petals; tack-stitch between the folds around the outer edge. Anchor knot the thread into the crinoline.

Finished flower

Urban Gardens

Picture elegant beds of flowering plants surrounded by well-manicured lawns,
or masterfully decorated pots surrounded by verdigris wrought-iron planters.
Among the beds and pots you will find these samples of favorite flowering beauties.

Most flowers listed in the following chart are accompanied by suggested leaf designs. In some cases, a leaf design is followed by a letter, indicating leaf size:

T = Tiny   **S** = Short   **M** = Medium   **L** = Long   **XL** = Extra-long

For instructions to make the leaves, see Petals and Greenery (page 120).

CHRYSANTHEMUM ... 66

⅜" satin ribbon

Triple Spear-Tip Leaf–S: ⅜" satin ribbon

CARNATION ... 67

½" and ⅜" satin ribbon

Lazy Loop Leaf–XL: ⅛" woven ombré ribbon

BLACK-EYED SUSAN ... 68

⅜" and ¼" satin ribbons

Lollypop Leaf: ⅝" satin ribbon

FORGET-ME-NOTS ... 68

¼" satin ribbon

Teardrop Leaf–M: ⅜" grosgrain ribbon

CLEMATIS ... 69

¼" satin and ⅛" grosgrain ribbons

Majestic Leaf–M: ½" satin ribbon

DIANTHUS ... 70

2 layers of ¼" satin ribbon

Lazy Loop Leaf–S: ¼" picot-edged ombré ribbon

WOOD ORCHID ... 71

2 layers of ½" satin ribbon

Thin Leaf: ⅛" satin ribbon

VERONICA ... 72

½" satin ribbon

Teardrop Leaf–S: ⅜" woven ombré ribbon

GERANIUM ... 73

⅝" silk bias ribbon

Jester's Leaf: ⅜" double-sided satin ribbon

DECORATIVE DAHLIA ... 74

⅝" satin ribbon

Spanish Leaf–L: ⅝" satin ribbon

RANUNCULUS ... 75

3 layers of ½" satin ribbon

Crown Leaf: ⅜" satin ribbon

AZALEA ... 76

⅜" satin ribbon

Elizabethan Leaf–M: ⅜" satin ribbon

ANEMONE ... 77

⅜" satin and grosgrain ribbon

Fleur-de-Lis Leaf: ⅝" woven ribbon

Chrysanthemum

Chrysanthemum and Triple Spear-Tip Leaf–S (page 132). Use same ribbon width for both flower and leaf.

SKILL LEVEL: *Intermediate* ●●

Suggested Ribbon

Woven ribbon with soft or medium hand, single- or double-sided

Amount needed:

- Approximately 76 × width of project ribbon, plus ½" *

Additional Supplies

- 3RW crinoline circle
- Second threaded needle

Measure

Ribbon width	Measure 2RW per petal.*
1"	2"
⅞"	1¾"
¾"	1½"
⅝"	1¼"
½"	1"
⅜"	¾"

* Do not cut the ribbon until instructed to do so.

DIRECTIONS

See General Instructions (page 28) and Ruched Petals (page 47).

1. Measure, pin, and gather stitch 38 ruched petals 2RW (see chart below left). Gently pull the thread tight to form the petals. Keep the needle threaded, and do not anchor or cut the thread.

2. Using the second needle, tackstitch the beginning raw edge to the crinoline.

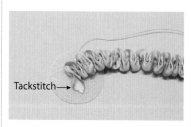

3. Tackstitch the centers of the first 5 petals in a spiral around the raw edges.

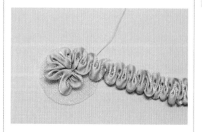

4. Tackstitch the centers of the remaining petals in a spiral around and under the center petals.

5. Tackstitch the raw edges of the last petal to the back of the crinoline. Anchor knot both threads to the crinoline.

Finished flower

Carnation

Carnation and Lazy Loop Leaf–XL (page 122). Use ribbon ¼″ narrower for leaf than for Color 2 of flower.

SKILL LEVEL: *Easy* ⬤

Suggested Ribbon

2 different widths and colors of woven ribbon with soft or medium hand, double-sided

Amount needed:

- **Color 1:** 36 × width of wider ribbon
- **Color 2:** 36 × width of wider ribbon (Use ⅛″ narrower ribbon for Color 2, cut same length as Color 1.)

Additional Supplies

- 2RW (of wider ribbon) crinoline circle
- 5 folded stamens

DIRECTIONS

See General Instructions (page 28), Layering Ribbon (page 16), and Rosette (page 35).

1. Whipstitch the stamens to the center of the crinoline. If needed, trim the ends of the stamens even with the edge of the crino-line circle.

2. Inner layer: Cut 1 length of ribbon from each color (see chart below). Follow the directions for layering; then follow the directions for the rosette up through pulling the gather thread, but do not anchor knot.

3. Insert the stamens through the opening of the inner layer; pull the thread tight to close the opening. Tackstitch the center gathers to the crinoline. Anchor knot and cut off the excess thread.

4. Outer layer: Cut 1 length of ribbon from each color (see chart below left). Follow the directions given in Step 2 for the inner layer. Fit the outer layer under the inner layer and on top of the crinoline.

5. From the wrong side, whipstitch the gathers to the crinoline. Anchor knot the thread.

Finished flower

Measure and Cut

Width of wider ribbon	Inner layer: Cut 1 length of each color.	Outer layer: Cut 1 length of each color.
1″	12″	24″
⅞″	10½″	21″
¾″	9″	18″
⅝″	7½″	15″
½″	6″	12″
⅜″	4½″	9″
¼″	3″	6″

Black-Eyed Susan

Black-Eyed Susan and Lollypop Leaf (page 126). Use ribbon ¼" wider for leaf than for flower.

SKILL LEVEL: *Easy* ◍

Suggested Ribbon

2 different widths and colors of woven or French wire ribbon with soft or medium hand, double-sided

Amount needed:

▪ **Flower:** Approximately 15 × width of Color 1 ribbon, plus ½" *

▪ **Center:** 13 × width of Color 2 ribbon (Use ¼" narrower ribbon than Color 1.)

Measure and Cut

Flower		Center	
Ribbon width	Measure 3RW per petal.*	Ribbon width	Cut 1 length 13RW.
1"	3"	¾"	9¾"
⅞"	2⅝"	⅝"	8⅛"
¾"	2¼"	½"	6½"
⅝"	1⅞"	⅜"	4⅞"
½"	1½"	¼"	3¼"
⅜"	1⅛"	⅛"	1⅝"

* Do not cut the ribbon until instructed to do so.

DIRECTIONS

See General Instructions (page 28), U-Gather Petals (page 43), and Ribbon Button (page 145).

1. Flower: Measure, pin, and stitch a 5-petal U-gather flower 3RW (see chart below). Cut the thread.

2. Center: Cut 1 length of ribbon 13RW (see chart below). Follow the directions for the ribbon button, but do not cut the thread. Stitch the center into the middle of the flower. Tackstitch and anchor knot the thread into the raw edges.

Finished flowers

Forget-Me-Nots

Forget-Me-Nots and Teardrop Leaf–M (page 129). Use ribbon ¼" wider for leaf than for flower.

SKILL LEVEL: *Easy* ◍

Suggested Ribbon

Woven or French wire ribbon with soft or medium hand, double-sided

Amount needed:

▪ Approximately 75 × width of project ribbon, plus 2½" *

Additional Supplies

▪ 1 piece of crinoline, large enough to fit group of 5 flowers

▪ Silk embroidery ribbon

DIRECTIONS

1. Follow Step 1 for black-eyed Susan (above left). Refer to the black-eyed Susan chart for measuring and cutting lengths. Make 5 flowers.

2. Tackstitch these flowers to the crinoline with the leaves. Using the silk embroidery ribbon, stitch a small French knot (page 30) into the center of each flower.

Clematis

Clematis and Majestic Leaf–M (page 131). Use ribbon ¼″ wider for leaf than for flower.

SKILL LEVEL: *Intermediate*

Suggested Ribbon

2 different widths and colors of woven or French wire ribbon with medium hand, double-sided

Amount needed:

■ **Petals:** 30 × width of Color 1 ribbon

■ **Center:** 6 × width of Color 2 ribbon (Use ⅛″ narrower ribbon than Color 1.)

Measure and Cut

Petal		Center	
Ribbon width	Cut 6 lengths 5RW.	Ribbon width	Cut 1 length 6RW.
1″	5″	⅞″	5¼″
⅞″	4⅜″	¾″	4½″
¾″	3¾″	⅝″	3¾″
⅝″	3⅛″	½″	3″
½″	2½″	⅜″	2¼″
⅜″	1⅞″	¼″	1½″
¼″	1¼″	⅛″	¾″

DIRECTIONS

See General Instructions (page 28); Pinwheel Leaf, Petal, or Bud (page 123); Individual-Petal Flower (page 48); and Knot Center (page 122).

1. Petals: Cut 6 lengths of ribbon 5RW (see chart below). For each length, follow the folding directions for the pinwheel petal; do not overlap the raw edges. Insert a pin through the raw edges of each ribbon.

2. Flower: Follow the gather-stitch directions for the individual-petal flower. Gently pull the thread to form the middle of the flower.

3. Center: Cut 1 length of ribbon 6RW (see chart below left). Tie an overhand knot in the ribbon. Insert the raw edges of the center into the middle of the flower; pull the thread of the petals tight to close the opening. Tackstitch and anchor knot the thread through the raw edges.

Finished flower

Dianthus

Dianthus and Lazy Loop Leaf–S (page 122). Use same ribbon width for both flower and leaf.

SKILL LEVEL: *Intermediate*

Suggested Ribbon

2 different colors of woven ribbon with soft or medium hand, single- or double-sided

Amount needed:

- **Flower:** 27 × width of Color 1 ribbon

- **Flower and center:** 33 × width of Color 2 ribbon

Additional Supplies

- 1RW × 8" strip of cardstock

DIRECTIONS

See General Instructions (page 28); Spiral-Loop Petals (page 45); and Knot Center (page 122).

1. Flower: Cut 1 length of ribbon 27RW from each color (see chart below). Place the lighter color on top. Follow the gather-stitch directions for making spiral-loop petals, stitching through both layers of ribbon.

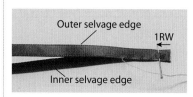

Outer selvage edge

1RW

Inner selvage edge

2. Evenly and very loosely loop the ribbon 5 times over the card-stock; the heads of the pins should be facing the same direction.

3. Follow the remaining gather-stitch directions for spiral-loop petals. Gently pull the thread to form the petals of the flower.

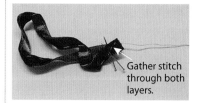

Gather stitch through both layers.

4. Center: Cut 1 length of ribbon 6RW from Color 2 (see chart below left); tie an overhand knot in the ribbon. Insert the raw edges of the center into the middle of the flower; pull the thread tight to close the opening. Tackstitch and anchor knot the thread into the raw edges.

Finished flower

Measure and Cut

Ribbon width	Flower: Cut 1 length 27RW from both colors.	Center: Cut 1 length 6RW from Color 2.
1"	27"	6"
⅞"	23⅝"	5¼"
¾"	20¼"	4½"
⅝"	16⅞"	3¾"
½"	13½"	3"
⅜"	10⅛"	2¼"
¼"	6¾"	1½"

Wood Orchid

Wood Orchid and Thin Leaf (page 132). Use ribbon ⅜" narrower for leaf than for outer petals of flower.

SKILL LEVEL: *Intermediate* 🌿🌿

Suggested Ribbon

2 different colors of woven or French wire ribbon with medium hand, single- or double-sided

Amount needed:

- **Inner petals:** 9 × width of Color 1 ribbon
- **Outer petals:** 12 × width of Color 2 ribbon

DIRECTIONS

See General Instructions (page 28); Trillium (page 54); Elizabethan Leaf, Petal, or Bud (page 125); and Individual-Petal Flower (page 48).

1. Inner petals: Cut 3 lengths of ribbon 3RW (see chart below). Follow the directions for the trillium, without the stamens; cut the thread.

2. Outer petals: Cut 3 lengths of ribbon 4RW (see chart below). For each length, follow the directions for an Elizabethan Petal through stitching the selvage edges. Cut the thread and open the petals flat.

3. Follow the gather-stitch directions for the individual-petal flower. Gently pull the thread to form the middle of the flower.

4. Insert the raw edges of the inner petals into the middle of the outer petals; pull the thread tight to close the opening. Tackstitch through the raw edges and anchor knot the thread.

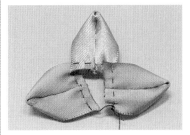

Finished flower. *Detail option:* medium French knot (page 30) or bead (page 32)

Measure and Cut

Ribbon width	Inner petals: Cut 3 lengths 3RW.	Outer petals: Cut 3 lengths 4RW.
1"	3"	4"
⅞"	2⅝"	3½"
¾"	2¼"	3"
⅝"	1⅞"	2½"
½"	1½"	2"
⅜"	1⅛"	1½"

Veronica

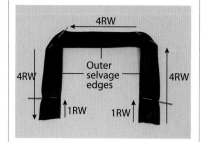

Veronica and Teardrop Leaf–S (page 129). Use ribbon ⅛″ narrower for leaf than for flower.

SKILL LEVEL: *Easy* 🌢

Suggested Ribbon

Woven or French wire ribbon with medium hand, double-sided

Amount needed:

- Approximately 14 × width of project ribbon*

Additional Supplies

- 3 folded stamens

Measure

Ribbon width	Measure 4RW per petal.*
1″	4″
⅞″	3½″
¾″	3″
⅝″	2½″
½″	2″
⅜″	1½″

Do not cut the ribbon until instructed to do so.

DIRECTIONS

See General Instructions (page 28) and Folded Petals (page 41).

1. Measure and pin 3 folded petals 4RW (see chart below left). Cut the excess ribbon. Insert a pin 1RW from each raw edge.

2. Anchor knot the thread into the inner selvage edge next to the first pin. Follow the gather-stitch directions for the folded petals just to the last pin.

3. Fold the ribbon in half, right side in, matching the raw edges. Gather stitch through both layers of ribbon diagonally toward the point on the outer selvage edges that is ⅛″ from the outer raw edges.

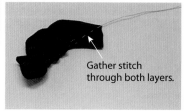

Gather stitch through both layers.

4. Gently pull the thread to form the petals; the raw edges will curve up. Insert the stamens through the opening of the flower. Pull the thread tight to close the opening. Tackstitch and anchor knot the thread through the raw edges.

Finished flower

Geranium

Geranium and Jester's Leaf (page 130). Use approximate folded width of flower ribbon for leaf ribbon width.

SKILL LEVEL: *Easy* 🝂

Suggested Ribbon

Silk bias ribbon: habotai, satin, or velvet

Amount needed:

- Approximately 30 × width of project ribbon, plus 1½″ *

Additional Supplies

- 1 square of crinoline, large enough to fit group of 3 flowers

DIRECTIONS

See General Instructions (page 28), U-Gather Petals (page 43), and Jester's Leaf (page 130). Where the directions for U-gather petals refer to the outer selvage edge, that will be the folded edge in this flower; the U-gather inner selvage edge will be the bias edge in this flower.

1. Flowers: Measure and pin 3 lengths of ribbon 10RW plus ½″ each (see chart below); do not cut the ribbon yet. Fold and gently finger-press the width of the ribbon in half. On the first length of ribbon, measure, pin, and gather stitch a 5-petal flower with 2RW (see chart below) U-gather petals; cut the thread and the ribbon. Repeat for the remaining lengths of ribbon to make 3 flowers.

2. Leaf: Make 1 jester's leaf (page 130).

3. Tackstitch the leaf and then the middle of each flower to the crinoline; anchor knot the thread. Cut off any excess crinoline.

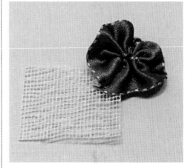

Finished flowers. *Detail option:* 5 small French knots (page 30) or beads (page 32)

Measure

Ribbon width	Measure 3 lengths 10RW plus ½″.*	Measure 2RW per petal.*
1″	10½″	2″
¾″	8″	1½″
⅝″	6¾″	1¼″
½″	5½″	1″
⁷⁄₁₆″	4⅞″	⅞″

* Do not cut the ribbon until instructed to do so.

Decorative Dahlia

Decorative Dahlia and Spanish Leaf–L (page 128). Use same ribbon width for both flower and leaf.

SKILL LEVEL: *Intermediate* 🌿🌿

Suggested Ribbon

Woven ribbon with soft or medium hand, double-sided

Amount needed:

- Approximately 42 × width of project ribbon, plus ½" *

Additional Supplies

- 2RW crinoline circle

Measure

Ribbon width	Measure 3RW per petal.*
1"	3"
⅞"	2⅝"
¾"	2¼"
⅝"	1⅞"
½"	1½"
⅜"	1⅛"

* Do not cut the ribbon until instructed to do so.

DIRECTIONS

See General Instructions (page 28) and Ruched Petals (page 47).

1. Measure, pin, and stitch a 14-petal ruched petal flower with 3RW petals (see chart above). Pull the thread tight to raise the center petals; anchor knot the thread. Pass the needle through the center of the crinoline; anchor knot the thread. The center petals should be facing up.

2. Tackstitch the middle of each bottom petal to the crinoline. Trim the crinoline and anchor knot the thread.

Finished flower. *Detail option:* small button (page 32)

Ranunculus

Ranunculus and Crown Leaf (page 133). Use ribbon ⅛″ narrower for leaf than for flower.

SKILL LEVEL: *Intermediate* 🌢🌢

Suggested Ribbon

3 different colors of woven ribbon with soft or medium hand, single- or double-sided

Amount needed:

- **Center:** 6 × width of Color 1 ribbon

- **Middle layer:** 8 × width of Color 2 ribbon

- **Outer layer:** 10 × width of Color 3 ribbon

Additional Supplies

- Second threaded needle

Measure and Cut

DIRECTIONS

See General Instructions (page 28) and Woven and Silk Bias Berries (page 149).

1. Center: Cut 1 length of ribbon 6RW (see chart below). Follow the directions for the stuffed woven berry. Anchor knot but do not cut the thread.

2. Middle layer: Cut 1 length of ribbon 8RW (see chart below). Follow the directions for the woven berry through the outer gather stitching. Insert the center into the middle layer. Using the first needle, tackstitch and anchor knot the center into the middle layer; cut this thread.

3. Gently pull the thread of the middle layer to fit snugly around the center; tackstitch the middle layer to the center around the selvage edge. Pull the needle through to the center of the middle layer; anchor knot and cut the thread.

4. Outer layer: Cut 1 length of ribbon 10RW (see chart below left). Follow the directions for the middle layer.

Finished flower

Ribbon width	Center: Cut 1 length 6RW.	Middle layer: Cut 1 length 8RW.	Outer layer: Cut 1 length 10RW.
1″	6″	8″	10″
⅞″	5¼″	7″	8¾″
¾″	4½″	6″	7½″
⅝″	3¾″	5″	6¼″
½″	3″	4″	5″
⅜″	2¼″	3″	3¾″

Azalea

Azalea and Elizabethan Leaf–M (page 125). Use same ribbon width for flower and leaf.

SKILL LEVEL: *Advanced* ●●●

Suggested Ribbon

Woven ribbon with soft or medium hand, double-sided

Amount needed:

- 27 × width of project ribbon

Additional Supplies

- 5 folded stamens

Measure and Cut

Ribbon width	Cut 3 lengths 9RW.
1"	9"
⅞"	7⅞"
¾"	6¾"
⅝"	5⅝"
½"	4½"
⅜"	3⅜"
¼"	2¼"

DIRECTIONS

See General Instructions (page 28) and Country Heart (page 140).

1. Petals: Cut 3 lengths of ribbon 9RW (see chart below left). Follow the directions for the country heart for each length; 1 length forms 1 group of petals.

2. Flower: Match the right sides, tips, and 1 lobe each of 2 groups of petals. Whipstitch from the tip to 1RW up the edge. Anchor knot and cut the thread.

3. Place the last group of petals on top of 1 lobe of the previous group. Whipstitch these 2 lobes together.

4. Whipstitch the remaining 2 lobes together. Insert the stamens through the opening in the middle of the flower.

5. Tackstitch through the tips to close the opening and hold the stamen in place; anchor knot the thread.

Finished flower

Anemone

Anemone and Fleur-de-Lis Leaf (page 127). Use ribbon ¼" wider for leaf than for flower.

SKILL LEVEL: *Intermediate* ●●

Suggested Ribbon

2 colors of woven or French wire ribbon with medium hand, double-sided

Amount needed:

■ **Flower:** Approximately 54 × width of Color 1 ribbon*

■ **Center:** 6 × width of Color 2 ribbon

Additional Supplies

■ 2RW × 8" strip of cardstock

DIRECTIONS

See General Instructions (page 28); Pinwheel Leaf, Petal, or Bud (page 123); Bias-Loop Petals (page 46); and Rosette (page 35).

1. Flower: Measure a length of ribbon 54RW (see chart below). Insert a pin 1RW in from the raw edge. Fold a pinwheel petal and pin it to the cardstock.

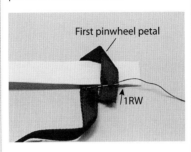

2. Fold and pin 7 more pinwheel petals. Measure an additional 1RW, and cut off the excess ribbon; insert a pin through the last petal.

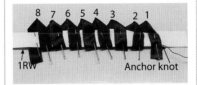

3. Follow the gather-stitch and assembly directions for bias-loop petals; cut the thread.

4. Center: Cut 1 length of ribbon 6RW (see chart below left). Follow the directions for a rosette; do not cut the thread. Place the center over the middle of the flower. Tackstitch the outer selvage edge of the center through the petals of the flower. Anchor knot the thread into the raw edges.

Finished flower

Measure and Cut

Ribbon width	Flower: Measure 1 length 54RW.*	Center: Cut 1 length 6RW.
1"	54"	6"
⅞"	47¼"	5¼"
¾"	40½"	4½"
⅝"	33¾"	3¾"
½"	27"	3"
⅜"	20¼"	2¼"

* Do not cut the ribbon until instructed to do so.

Grandmothers' Gardens

Are you remembering the plot set along the fence or next to the shed?
Such energetic, robust gardens full of glorious color can only be found in the
English countryside—or your grandmother's garden.

Most flowers listed in the following chart are accompanied by suggested leaf designs. In some cases, a leaf design is followed by a letter, indicating leaf size:

T = Tiny   **S** = Short   **M** = Medium   **L** = Long   **XL** = Extra-long

For instructions to make the leaves, see Petals and Greenery (page 120).

CROCUS ... 80
⅝" French wire ribbon
Lazy Loop Leaf–L: ¼" picot-edged ombré ribbon

ASTER ... 86
¼" picot-edged ombré and ⅛" woven ribbons
Elizabethan Leaf–S: ⅝" taffeta ribbon

NARCISSUS ... 81
1" silk bias ribbon
Elizabethan Leaf–L: ½" woven ribbon

VINE FLOWER ... 87
½" satin ribbon
Edwardian Leaf–M: ⅝" satin ribbon

MAID'S CAP ... 82
⅝" and ⅜" satin ribbons
Parisian Leaf–S: ⅜" satin ribbon

MALLOW ... 88
½" satin and ⅜" grosgrain ribbons
Fleur-de-Lis Leaf: ¾" satin ribbon

CATHEDRAL BELLS ... 83
1" silk bias ribbon
Rounded Leaf–M: 1" silk bias ribbon

CAMELLIA ... 89
⅝" satin ribbon
Victorian Leaf–L: ⅝" satin ribbon

HOLLYHOCK ... 84
⅜" grosgrain and ¼" picot-edged ombré ribbons
Fleur-de-Lis Leaf: ⅝" satin ribbon

CONEFLOWER ... 90
⅜" grosgrain ribbon
Spear-Tip Leaf–L: ⅜" satin ribbon

SWEET PEA ... 85
½" satin and ⅜" grosgrain ribbons
Twin Elizabethan Leaf–S: ⅜" satin ribbon

BEARDED IRIS ... 91
⅝" satin ribbon
Iris Leaf: ⅝" satin ribbon

Crocus

Crocus and Lazy Loop Leaf–L (page 122). Use ribbon ⅜" narrower for leaf than for flower.

SKILL LEVEL: *Intermediate* ◗◗

Suggested Ribbon

1-color version: Ombré or variegated ribbon (reverse the colors between inner and outer layers of petals)

2-color version: 2 different colors of woven or French wire ribbon with soft or medium hand, single- or double-sided

Amount needed:

- **1-color version:** 18 × width of ombré or variegated ribbon

- **2-color version:** 9 × width of each color of woven ribbons

Measure and Cut

Ribbon width	Cut 6 lengths 3RW.*
1″	3″
⅞″	2⅝″
¾″	2¼″
⅝″	1⅞″
½″	1½″
⅜″	1⅛″

* If using 2 colors, cut 3 lengths from each color.

DIRECTIONS

See General Instructions (page 28) and Trillium (page 54).

1. If using an ombré or variegated ribbon: Cut 6 lengths of ribbon 3RW (see chart above); reverse the colors between the inner and outer layers.

If using 2 different colors of woven ribbon: Cut 3 lengths of ribbon from each color, all at 3RW (see chart above).

Inner layer: Follow the trillium assembly directions to make 3 petals in the lighter color (either with the ombré or variegated ribbon turned so the colors look lighter, or using the lighter of the 2 colors of woven ribbon). Cut the thread.

2. Outer layer: Follow the directions of the trillium through the gather stitching with the remaining 3 (darker) lengths of ribbon.

3. Insert the raw edges of the inner layer into the middle of the outer layer. Gently pull the thread to close the opening. Tackstitch through the raw edges and anchor knot the thread.

Finished flower. *Detail option:* 3 small French knots (page 30) or beads (page 32)

Narcissus

Narcissus and Elizabethan Leaf–L (page 125). Use folded width of flower ribbon for leaf ribbon width.

SKILL LEVEL: *Intermediate* ⬤⬤

Suggested Ribbon

2 different colors of silk bias ribbon: habotai or satin

Amount needed:

■ **Petals:** 12 × width of Color 2 ribbon

■ **Center:** 4 × width of Color 1 ribbon

Measure and Cut

Ribbon width	Petals: Cut 6 lengths 2RW.	Center: Cut 1 length 4RW.
1″	2″	4″
¾″	1½″	3″
⅝″	1¼″	2½″
½″	1″	2″
⁷⁄₁₆″	⅞″	1¾″

DIRECTIONS

See General Instructions (page 28); Simple Leaf, Petal, or Bud (page 125); Individual-Petal Flower (page 48); and Folded-Edge Rosette (page 37).

1. Petals: Cut 6 lengths of ribbon 2RW (see chart below left). Follow the directions for the simple petal for each length; cut the thread.

2. Flower: Follow the directions for the individual-petal flower with the raw edges of the petals meeting in the center. Do not cut the thread.

3. Center: Follow the directions for the folded-edge rosette. Stitch the thread to the outer fold; gather stitch around and through the folded edges. Do not cut the thread.

4. Stitch the center to the middle of the flower using the thread from the petals. Anchor knot the thread into the raw edges; cut the thread. Gently pull the thread from the center to slightly close the opening. Tackstitch the side of the center to the petals. Anchor knot the thread into the raw edges of the flower.

Finished flower

Maid's Cap

Maid's Cap and Parisian Leaf–S (page 123). Use same ribbon width for both outer petals and leaf.

SKILL LEVEL: *Intermediate* ◗ ◗

Suggested Ribbon

2 different widths and colors of woven ribbon with soft or medium hand, single- or double-sided.

Amount needed:

- **Center:** 10 × width of Color 1 ribbon (Use ¼" wider ribbon than for petals.)
- **Petals:** Approximately 24 × width of Color 2 ribbon, plus ½" *

Additional Supplies

- 2RW (of petal ribbon) crinoline circle

Measure and Cut

Center		Petals	
Ribbon width	Cut 1 length 10RW.	Ribbon width	Measure 2RW per petal.*
1⅛"	11¼"	⅞"	1¾"
1"	10"	¾"	1½"
⅞"	8¾"	⅝"	1¼"
¾"	7½"	½"	1"
⅝"	6¼"	⅜"	¾"

* Do not cut the ribbon until instructed to do so.

DIRECTIONS

See General Instructions (page 28), Woven and Silk Bias Berries (page 149), and Ruched Petals (page 47).

1. Center: Cut 1 length of ribbon 10RW (see chart above). Follow the assembly directions for the stuffed woven berry. Stitch the center to the middle of the crinoline; cut the thread.

2. Petals: Measure, pin, and gather stitch 12 ruched petals 2RW (see chart above). Gently pull the thread to form the petals; the inner petals should just fit under the center. Follow the remaining ruched petal directions to finish the flower.

3. Tackstitch the raw edges to the back of the crinoline. Tackstitch the center petals to the crinoline; anchor knot the thread.

Tackstitch

Finished flower. *Detail option:* medium French knot (page 30) or bead (page 32)

Cathedral Bells

Cathedral Bells and Rounded Leaf–M (page 137). Use same ribbon width for flower and leaf.

SKILL LEVEL: *Intermediate*

Suggested Ribbon

Silk bias habotai ribbon

Amount needed:

- 10 × width of project ribbon

Measure and Cut

Ribbon width	Cut 1 length 10RW.
1″	10″
¾″	7½″
⅝″	6¼″
½″	5″
⁷⁄₁₆″	4⅜″

DIRECTIONS

See General Instructions (page 28) and Double-Edge Rosette (page 36).

1. Cut 1 length of ribbon 10RW (see chart below left). Fold and gently finger-press the width of the ribbon to three-fourths the original width.

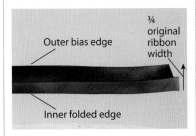

¾ original ribbon width

Outer bias edge

Inner folded edge

2. Follow the seam and gather-stitch directions for the double-edge rosette, with the folded side out. Gently pull the thread to form the middle of the flower. Anchor knot the thread through the raw edges.

3. Tackstitch the thread to the inner bias edge. Gather stitch around the inner bias edge through both layers of ribbon.

4. Pull the thread tight to form the middle of the flower. Tackstitch into the raw edges and anchor knot the thread.

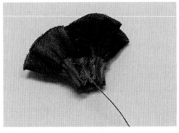

Finished flower

Hollyhock

Hollyhock and Fleur-de-Lis Leaf (page 127). Use ribbon ¼" wider for leaf than for flower.

SKILL LEVEL: *Intermediate* ● ●

Suggested Ribbon

2 different widths and colors of woven ribbon with soft or medium hand, double-sided

Amount needed:

■ **Center:** 8 × width of Color 1 ribbon

■ **Flower:** 32 × width of Color 2 ribbon (Use ⅛" wider ribbon than for center.)

Additional Supplies

■ 1RW × 8" strip of cardstock

Measure and Cut

Center		Flower	
Ribbon width	Cut 1 length 8RW.	Ribbon width	Cut 1 length 32RW.
⅞"	7"	1"	32"
¾"	6"	⅞"	28"
⅝"	5"	¾"	24"
½"	4"	⅝"	20"
⅜"	3"	½"	16"
¼"	2"	⅜"	12"

DIRECTIONS

See General Instructions (page 28), Rosette (page 35), and Spiral-Loop Petals (page 45).

1. Center: Cut 1 length of ribbon 8RW (see chart above). Follow the directions for the rosette; cut the thread.

2. Flower: Cut 1 length of ribbon 32RW (see chart above). Follow the directions for spiral-loop petals, evenly and loosely looping the ribbon 6 times over the card-stock. When the spiral-loop flower is complete, do not cut the thread.

3. Tackstitch the center into the middle of the flower. Anchor knot the thread through the raw edges.

Finished flower. *Detail option:* large French knot (page 30) or bead (page 32)

Sweet Pea

Sweet Pea and Twin Elizabethan Leaf–S (page 134). Use same ribbon width for flower and leaf.

SKILL LEVEL: *Intermediate* 🌿🌿

Suggested Ribbon

2 different widths and colors of woven or French wire ribbon with soft or medium hand, double-sided

Amount needed:

- **Center:** 4 × width of Color 1 ribbon (Use ⅛" wider ribbon than for flower.)

- **Flower:** 9 × width of Color 2 ribbon

DIRECTIONS

See General Instructions (page 28), Half U-Gather Petals (page 148), and Country Heart (page 140).

1. Center: Cut 1 length of ribbon 4RW (see chart below). Follow the directions for the half U-gather petal; cut the thread.

2. Flower: Cut 1 length of ribbon 9RW (see chart below). Follow the fold, seam, and gather-stitch directions for the country heart. Gently pull the thread to form the middle of the flower. Do not cut the thread.

3. Insert the raw edges of the center through the middle of the flower; pull the thread tight to close the opening. Tackstitch the raw edges of the center to the flower; anchor knot the thread.

Finished flower

Measure and Cut

Center		Flower	
Ribbon width	Cut 1 length 4RW.	Ribbon width	Cut 1 length 9RW.
1"	4"	⅞"	7⅞"
⅞"	3½"	¾"	6¾"
¾"	3"	⅝"	5⅝"
⅝"	2½"	½"	4½"
½"	2"	⅜"	3⅜"
⅜"	1½"	¼"	2¼"

Aster

Aster and Elizabethan Leaf–S (page 125). Use ribbon ⅜″ wider for leaf than for center.

SKILL LEVEL: *Intermediate* ◗◗

Suggested Ribbon

2 different widths and colors of woven ribbon with soft or medium hand, double-sided.

Amount needed:

- **Center:** 6 × width of Color 1 ribbon (Use ⅛″ wider ribbon than for petals.)
- **Petals:** 56 × width of Color 2 ribbon

Additional Supplies

Square of crinoline with a circle drawn on it the same size as the finished center.

Measure and Cut

Center		Petals	
Ribbon width	Cut 1 length 6RW.	Ribbon width	Cut 8 lengths 7RW.
1″	6″	⅞″	6⅛″
⅞″	5¼″	¾″	5¼″
¾″	4½″	⅝″	4⅜″
⅝″	3¾″	½″	3½″
½″	3″	⅜″	2⅝″
⅜″	2¼″	¼″	1¾″
¼″	1½″	⅛″	⅞″

DIRECTIONS

See General Instructions (page 28) and Rosette (page 35).

1. Center: Cut 1 length of ribbon 6RW (see chart above). Stitch a rosette. Cut the thread.

2. Petals: Cut 8 lengths of ribbon 7RW (see chart above). Tackstitch 1 raw edge to the crinoline, ⅛″ in from the outer edge of the circle.

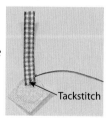

Tackstitch

3. Fold the petal in half, flipping the remaining raw edge back to the crinoline. Overlap the first raw edge and tackstitch to the crinoline.

Tackstitch

4. Stitch each petal in place. Anchor knot the thread into the crinoline; cut away the excess crinoline. Do not cut the thread.

5. Place the center over the middle of the flower. Tackstitch the outer selvage edge of the center through the petals of the flower. Anchor knot the thread into the crinoline.

Finished flower. *Detail option:* large French knot (page 30) or bead (page 32)

Vine Flower

Vine Flower and Edwardian Leaf—M (page 129). Use same ribbon width for both flower and leaf.

SKILL LEVEL: *Intermediate*

Suggested Ribbon

2 different colors of woven ribbon with soft or medium hand, double-sided

Amount needed:

■ **Flower:** Approximately 7 × width of Color 1 ribbon*

■ **Bud cap:** 6 × width of Color 2 ribbon

Additional Supplies

■ 3 folded stamens

■ Second threaded needle

Measure and Cut

Ribbon width	Flower: Measure 3RW per petal.*	Bud cap: Cut 1 length 6RW.
1″	3″	6″
⅞″	2⅝″	5¼″
¾″	2¼″	4½″
⅝″	1⅞″	3¾″
½″	1½″	3″
⅜″	1⅛″	2¼″

* Do not cut the ribbon until instructed to do so.

DIRECTIONS

See General Instructions (page 28), Two-Petal Flower (page 42), and Bud Cap (page 136).

1. Flower: Measure and pin a two-petal flower 3RW (see chart above). Follow the gather-stitch directions and gently pull the thread to form the petals.

2. Insert the stamens through the opening of the flower; pull the thread tight to close the opening. Tackstitch and anchor knot the thread into the raw edges; do not cut the thread.

3. Bud cap: Cut 1 length of ribbon 6RW (see chart above). Using the second needle, follow the directions for the bud cap through the outer gather stitching.

4. Insert the first needle through the center of the cap; pull the flower into the cap. Follow the remaining directions.

Finished flower

Mallow

Mallow and Fleur-de-Lis Leaf (page 127). Use ribbon ¼" wider for leaf than for petals.

SKILL LEVEL: *Intermediate*

Suggested Ribbon

2 different widths and colors of woven ribbon with medium hand, double-sided

Amount needed:

- **Petals:** 40 × width of Color 1 ribbon

- **Center:** 6 × width of Color 2 ribbon (Use ⅛" narrower ribbon than for petals.)

DIRECTIONS

See General Instructions (page 28); Parisian Leaf, Petal, or Bud (page 123); Individual-Petal Flower (page 48); and Knot Center (page 122).

1. Petals: Cut 5 lengths of ribbon 8RW (see chart below). Tie an overhand knot into the center of each length.

2. Follow the directions for the Parisian petal for each length; cut the thread.

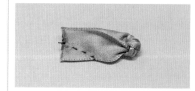

3. Flower: Follow the gather-stitch directions for the individual-petal flower. Gently pull the thread to form the middle of the flower.

4. Center: Cut 1 length of ribbon 6RW (see chart below left); tie an overhand knot into the center of the length. Insert the raw edges of the center into the middle of the flower; pull the thread tight to close the opening. Tackstitch the raw edges of the center to the raw edges of the flower; anchor knot the thread.

Finished flower

Measure and Cut

Petals		Center	
Ribbon width	Cut 5 lengths 8RW.	Ribbon width	Cut 1 length 6RW.
1"	8"	⅞"	5¼"
⅞"	7"	¾"	4½"
¾"	6"	⅝"	3¾"
⅝"	5"	½"	3"
½"	4"	⅜"	2¼"
⅜"	3"	¼"	1½"

Camellia

Camellia and Victorian Leaf–L (page 130). Use same ribbon width for both flower and leaf.

SKILL LEVEL: **Advanced**

Suggested Ribbon

Woven or French wire ribbon with soft or medium hand, double-sided

Amount needed:

■ Approximately 46 × width of project ribbon*

Additional Supplies

■ 2RW crinoline circle

■ Second threaded needle

Measure

Ribbon width	Measure 2RW per petal.*
1″	2″
⅞″	1¾″
¾″	1½″
⅝″	1¼″
½″	1″
⅜″	¾″

* Do not cut the ribbon until instructed to do so.

DIRECTIONS

See General Instructions (page 28) and Folded Petals (page 41).

1. Measure 2RW (see chart below left) in from the raw edge; fold the ribbon forward at a 90° angle; fold forward again and insert a pin through the folds; this is 1 double-fold petal.

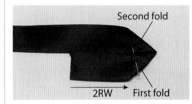

Second fold

2RW   First fold

2. Measure each of the next 10 double-fold petals from the last fold of the previous petal (for a total of 11 petals); then measure 2RW and cut off the excess ribbon.

3. Insert a pin 1RW from each raw edge. Follow the gather-stitch directions for making folded petals. Gently pull the thread to form the petals. Do not cut the thread.

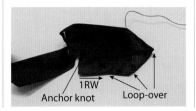

1RW
Anchor knot   Loop-over

4. Using the second needle, tackstitch the beginning raw edge to the center of the crinoline.

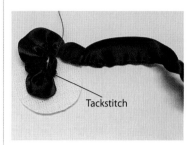

Tackstitch

5. Tackstitch the remaining petals in a spiral around and under the previous row of petals. Tuck the raw edge of the last petal under the previous row and stitch to the crinoline. Anchor knot both threads to the crinoline.

Finished flower

Coneflower

Coneflower and Spear-Tip Leaf–L (page 126). Use same ribbon width for petals and leaf.

SKILL LEVEL: *Intermediate* 🌢🌢

Suggested Ribbon

2 different colors of woven ribbon with medium hand, single- or double-sided

Amount needed:

■ **Center:** 6 × width of Color 1 ribbon

■ **Petals:** 30 × width of Color 2 ribbon

Additional Supplies

■ Second threaded needle

Measure and Cut

Ribbon width	Center: Cut 1 length 6RW.	Petals: Cut 5 lengths 6RW.
1″	6″	6″
⅞″	5¼″	5¼″
¾″	4½″	4½″
⅝″	3¾″	3¾″
½″	3″	3″
⅜″	2¼″	2¼″

DIRECTIONS

See General Instructions (page 28); Bud Cap (page 136); and Spear-Tip Leaf, Petal, or Bud (page 126).

1. Center: Cut 1 length of ribbon 6RW (see chart below). Follow the directions for the bud cap through the outer gather stitching; keep the needle threaded, and do not anchor or cut the thread.

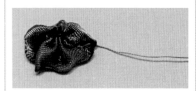

2. Petals: Cut 5 lengths of ribbon 6RW (see chart below). Using the second needle, follow the directions for the spear-tip petal for each length; cut the thread.

3. Flower: Anchor knot the thread into the selvage edge of the first petal. Stitch through the raw edges of each petal. Gently pull the thread tight; anchor knot the thread.

4. Insert the flower needle through the center of the bud cap; pull the petals into the cap. Follow the remaining directions for the bud cap.

Finished flower

Bearded Iris

Bearded Iris and Iris Leaf (page 131). Use same ribbon width for both flower and leaf.

SKILL LEVEL: *Advanced* ●●●

Suggested Ribbon

2 different colors of woven or French wire ribbon with medium hand, single- or double-sided

Amount needed:

■ **Center and side petals:**

13 × width of Color 1 ribbon

■ **Top and bottom petals:**

8 × width of Color 2 ribbon

DIRECTIONS

See General Instructions (page 28), Half U-Gather Petals (page 148), and Two-Petal Flower (page 42). Where the directions for Two-Petal Flower refer to the fold, that will be the layers of ribbon in this flower.

1. Center and side petals: Cut 1 length of ribbon 3RW for the center petal and 2 lengths of ribbon 5RW for the side petals (see chart below); work with 1 length at a time to make 3 petals. Follow the directions for the half U-gather petal; cut the thread from the center only.

2. Top and bottom petals: Cut 1 length of ribbon 5RW for the top petal and 1 length of ribbon 3RW for the bottom petal (see chart below left). Overlap and align the raw edge of the shorter petal with the selvage edge of the longer petal, right sides up. Insert a pin through the overlapped edges and also 1RW from each remaining raw edge. Follow the gather-stitch directions for the two-petal flower.

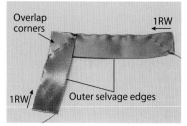

3. Gently pull the thread to form the petals. Insert the raw edges of the center through the middle of the flower; gently pull the thread to close the opening.

Measure and Cut

Ribbon width	Center and side petals		Top and bottom petals	
	Cut 1 length 3RW.	Cut 2 lengths 5RW.	Cut 1 length 5RW.	Cut 1 length 3RW.
1″	3″	5″	5″	3″
⅞″	2⅝″	4⅜″	4⅜″	2⅝″
¾″	2¼″	3¾″	3¾″	2¼″
⅝″	1⅞″	3⅛″	3⅛″	1⅞″
½″	1½″	2½″	2½″	1½″
⅜″	1⅛″	1⅞″	1⅞″	1⅛″

4. Match the raw edges. Tackstitch the raw edges of the center, top, and bottom petals together; cut the thread.

5. Side petals: Tackstitch the raw edge of a side petal to the raw edges of the flower.

6. Repeat Step 5 for the other side petal; anchor knot the thread.

Finished flower

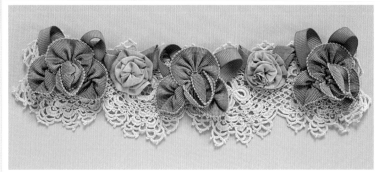

Begonia and Iris Cuff, 2½″ × 8½″

Enchanted Gardens

*It is said that if you want the fairies to visit, you should plant pansies in your garden.
Why not add these other charming blooms to entice the butterflies and all things magical?*

Most flowers listed in the following chart are accompanied by suggested leaf designs. In some cases, a leaf design is followed by a letter, indicating leaf size:

T = Tiny   **S** = Short   **M** = Medium   **L** = Long   **XL** = Extra-long

For instructions to make the leaves, see Petals and Greenery (page 120).

BEGONIA ... 95
⅝" silk bias ribbon

Arrowhead Leaf: ⅝" satin ribbon

BLEEDING HEART ... 101
⅝" and ½" satin ribbons

Victorian Leaf–M: ⅝" satin ribbon

PANSY ... 96
½" and ⅜" satin ribbons

Spanish Leaf–S: ⅝" satin ribbon

ORCHID ... 102
½" satin ribbon

Majestic Leaf–L: ⅜" satin ribbon

LUPINE ... 97
¼" satin ribbon

Triple Spear-Tip Leaf–S: ⅜" satin ribbon

PERSIAN VIOLET ... 103
¼" satin ribbon

Spanish Leaf–M: ⅝" satin ribbon

MORNING GLORY ... 98
1" silk bias ribbon

Morning Glory Leaf: 1" silk bias ribbon

FUCHSIA ... 104
⅝" and ½" satin ribbons

Elizabethan Leaf–L: ⅝" satin ribbon

STAR LILY ... 99
⅜" satin ribbon

Lazy Loop Leaf–XL: ¼" picot-edged woven ribbon

COSMOS ... 105
⅜" satin ribbon

Thin Leaf: ⅛" satin ribbon

ZINNIA ... 100
½" satin and ⅜" wire-edge ribbons

Twin Elizabethan Leaf–S: ⅜" ombré woven ribbon

JASMINE ... 106
⅜" satin ribbon

Victorian Leaf–M: ⅜" satin ribbon

Begonia

Begonia and Arrowhead Leaf (page 128). Use original ribbon width of flower for leaf ribbon width.

SKILL LEVEL: *Easy* ⬤

Suggested Ribbon

Silk bias ribbon: habotai, satin, or velvet (*Option:* Use 3 different colors of ribbon.)

Amount needed:

- **1-color version:** 24 × width of project ribbon
- **3-color version:**

    Inner layer: 6 × width of Color 1 ribbon

    Middle layer: 8 × width of Color 2 ribbon

    Outer layer: 10 × width of Color 3 ribbon

Additional Supplies

- 2RW crinoline circle

Measure and Cut

Ribbon width	Inner layer: Cut 1 length 6RW.	Middle layer: Cut 1 length 8RW.	Outer layer: Cut 1 length 10RW.
1"	6"	8"	10"
¾"	4½"	6"	7½"
⅝"	3¾"	5"	6¼"
½"	3"	4"	5"
⁷⁄₁₆"	2⅝"	3½"	4⅜"

DIRECTIONS

See General Instructions (page 28) and Folded-Edge Rosette (page 37).

1. Cut 1 each of the following ribbon lengths: 6RW, 8RW, and 10RW (see chart above). For each length, follow the folded-edge rosette directions through the gather stitching.

Inner layer: Gently pull the thread to form the center of the flower. Tackstitch the center of the inner layer to the crinoline; anchor knot and cut the thread.

2. Middle layer: Gently pull the thread to form the middle of the flower. Arrange the middle layer under the inner layer and on top of the crinoline.

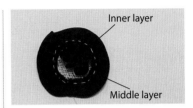

Inner layer

Middle layer

3. Gently pull the thread to close the opening. Tackstitch the center gathers to the crinoline; anchor knot and cut the thread.

4. Outer layer: Repeat Steps 2 and 3, as given for the middle layer.

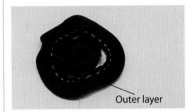

Outer layer

Finished flower

Pansy

Pansy and Spanish Leaf–S (page 128). Use ribbon ⅛″ wider for leaf than for lower (yellow) petals.

SKILL LEVEL: *Intermediate* 🌢🌢

Suggested Ribbon

2 different widths and colors of woven or French wire ribbon with medium hand, double-sided.

Amount needed:

- **Lower petals and center:** Approximately 20 × width of Color 1 ribbon*

- **Upper petals:** Approximately 9 × width of Color 2 ribbon* (Use ⅛″ wider ribbon than for lower petals and center.)

DIRECTIONS

See General Instructions (page 28), Folded Petals (page 41), Two-Petal Flower (page 42), and Knot Center (page 122).

1. Lower petals: Measure and pin a folded-petal flower, 3RW, 6RW, and 3RW (see chart below), with the folds facing inward. Follow the gather-stitch and assembly directions.

2. Center: Cut 1 length of ribbon 6RW (see chart below). Tie an overhand knot in the ribbon. Insert the raw edges of the center into the middle of the top-layer petals; pull the thread tight to close the opening. Tackstitch through the raw edges; cut the thread.

3. Upper petals: Measure and pin a two-petal flower 4RW (see chart below left). Follow the gather-stitch directions and gently pull the thread to form the petals.

4. Tackstitch the raw edges of the upper petals into the raw edges of the lower petals and anchor knot the thread.

Finished flower

Measure

Lower petals and center			Upper petals	
Ribbon width	Measure 3RW per petal.*	Measure 6RW.*	Ribbon width	Measure 4RW per petal.*
1″	3″	6″	1⅛″	4½″
⅞″	2⅝″	5¼″	1″	4″
¾″	2¼″	4½″	⅞″	3½″
⅝″	1⅞″	3¾″	¾″	3″
½″	1½″	3″	⅝″	2½″
⅜″	1⅛″	2¼″	½″	2″
¼″	¾″	1½″	⅜″	1½″

* Do not cut the ribbon until instructed to do so.

Lupine

Lupine and Triple Spear-Tip Leaf–S (page 132). Use ribbon ⅛" wider for leaf than for flower.

SKILL LEVEL: *Easy* ◗

Suggested Ribbon

Woven or French wire ribbon with soft or medium hand, double-sided

Amount needed:

- Approximately 40 × width of project ribbon*

Additional Supplies

- 1 rectangle of crinoline large enough for 5 flowers

DIRECTIONS

See General Instructions (page 28) and Two-Petal Flower (page 42).

1. Measure and pin 5 lengths of ribbon 8RW each (see chart below); do not cut the ribbon. On the first length of ribbon, measure and pin a two-petal flower, 3RW and 4RW (see chart below). Follow the two-petal flower gather-stitch and assembly directions, with the upper petal resting above the lower petal. Repeat for the remaining lengths of ribbon to make 5 flowers.

2. Tackstitch the middle of each flower to the crinoline; anchor knot the thread. If adding leaves, tackstitch them to the back of the crinoline.

Finished group of flowers

Measure

Ribbon width	Measure 5 lengths 8RW.*	Upper petal: Measure 3RW from each length at left.*	Lower petal: Measure 4RW from each length at left.*
1"	8"	3"	4"
⅞"	7"	2⅝"	3½"
¾"	6"	2¼"	3"
⅝"	5"	1⅞"	2½"
½"	4"	1½"	2"
⅜"	3"	1⅛"	1½"
¼"	2"	¾"	1"

* Do not cut the ribbon until instructed to do so.

Morning Glory

Morning Glory and Morning Glory Leaf (page 137). Use same ribbon width for both flower and leaf.

SKILL LEVEL: *Advanced* ◗◗◗

Suggested Ribbon

Silk bias ribbon: habotai or satin

Amount needed:

- 4 × width of project ribbon

Additional Supplies

- 1 folded stamen

Measure and Cut

Ribbon width	Cut 1 length 4RW.
1"	4"
¾"	3"
⅝"	2½"
½"	2"
⁷⁄₁₆"	1¾"

DIRECTIONS

See General Instructions (page 28) and Folded-Edge Rosette (page 37).

1. Cut 1 length of ribbon 4RW (see chart below left). Follow the directions for the folded-edge rosette through the seam; tack-stitch the folded width at the seam. Divide the finished circumference by 5. Insert a pin at the seam; measure and pin 4 sections from this point (5 petals total).

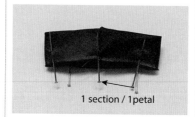

1 section / 1 petal

2. Work with 1 section at a time. Fold the ribbon in half at a pin. Remove the pin. Stitch a small dart through the layers of ribbon to the fold, using assembly stitch 1; stitch back to the bias edge. Anchor knot and cut the thread.

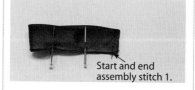

Start and end assembly stitch 1.

3. Repeat for each remaining pin. Do not cut the thread on the last dart.

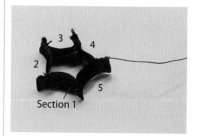

Section 1

4. Gather stitch around and through the bias edges and folded darts. Gently pull the thread to form the middle of the flower. Insert the folded stamen through the opening; pull the thread tight to close the middle. Anchor knot the thread through the raw edges.

Finished flower

Star Lily

Star Lily and Lazy Loop Leaf–XL (page 122). Use ribbon ⅛" narrower for leaf than for flower.

SKILL LEVEL: *Intermediate*

Suggested Ribbon

Woven or French wire ribbon with medium hand, single- or double-sided

Amount needed:

- 36 × width of project ribbon

Additional Supplies

- 3 folded stamens

Measure and Cut

Ribbon width	Cut 6 lengths 6RW.
1"	6"
⅞"	5¼"
¾"	4½"
⅝"	3¾"
½"	3"
⅜"	2¼"
¼"	1½"

DIRECTIONS

See General Instructions (page 28); Elizabethan Leaf, Petal, or Bud (page 125); and Individual-Petal Flower (page 48).

1. Cut 6 lengths of ribbon 6RW (see chart below left). Follow the directions for the Elizabethan petal, through the stitched selvage edges for each length; cut the thread.

2. Inner layer, 3 petals: Follow the directions for the individual-petal flower through the gather stitching. Stitch through the selvage edge next to the beginning anchor knot.

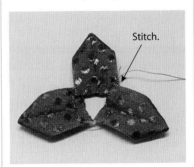

Stitch.

3. Gently pull the thread to form the middle of the flower. Insert the stamens; pull the thread tight to close the opening. Tackstitch and anchor knot through the raw edges; cut the thread.

4. Outer layer, 3 petals: Follow the directions for the inner layer, through the gather stitching. Insert the inner layer into the middle of the outer layer. Follow the remaining individual-petal flower directions.

Finished flower

Zinnia

Zinnia and Twin Elizabethan Leaf–S (page 134). Use same ribbon width for both flower and leaf.

SKILL LEVEL: *Intermediate*

Suggested Ribbon

2 different widths and colors of woven or French wire ribbon with soft or medium hand, double-sided

Amount needed:

■ **Center:** 6 × width of Color 1 ribbon (Use ⅛" wider ribbon than for petals.)

■ **Flower:** Approximately 33 × width of Color 2 ribbon*

Additional Supplies

■ 2RW (of flower ribbon) crinoline circle

Measure and Cut

Center		Flower	
Ribbon width	Cut 1 length 6RW.	Ribbon width	Measure 2RW per petal*
1"	6"	⅞"	1¾"
⅞"	5¼"	¾"	1½"
¾"	4½"	⅝"	1¼"
⅝"	3¾"	½"	1"
½"	3"	⅜"	¾"

*Do not cut the ribbon until instructed to do so.

DIRECTIONS

See General Instructions (page 28), Woven and Silk Bias Berries (page 149), and Camellia (page 89).

1. Center: Cut 1 length of ribbon 6RW (see chart above). Follow the directions for the woven berry. Stitch the center to the middle of the crinoline; cut the thread.

2. Flower: Follow the directions for the camellia; measure and pin 8 double-fold petals, 2RW per side (see chart above); measure 1RW after the last fold. Cut off the excess ribbon and gather stitch. Stitch through the selvage edge next to the beginning anchor knot. Gently pull the thread to form the petals around the center; the inner petals should just fit under the center.

3. Anchor knot the thread into the raw edges. Tackstitch the inner petal edge to the crinoline; anchor knot the thread.

Finished flower. *Detail option:* small French knots around outer edge of center (page 30)

Bleeding Heart

Bleeding Heart and Victorian Leaf–M (page 130). Use same ribbon width for petals and leaf.

SKILL LEVEL: *Easy* ◗

Suggested Ribbon

2 different widths and colors of woven or French wire ribbon with soft or medium hand; single- or double-sided

Amount needed:

- **Petals:** 8 × width of Color 1 ribbon

- **Center:** 4 × width of Color 2 ribbon (Use ⅛" wider ribbon than for petals.)

Measure and Cut

Petals		Center	
Ribbon width	Cut 1 length 8RW.	Ribbon width	Cut 1 length 4RW.
1"	8"	1⅛"	4½"
⅞"	7"	1"	4"
¾"	6"	⅞"	3½"
⅝"	5"	¾"	3"
½"	4"	⅝"	2½"
⅜"	3"	½"	2"
¼"	2"	⅜"	1½"

DIRECTIONS

See General Instructions (page 28), Posy (page 38), and Half U-Gather Petals (page 148).

1. Petals: Cut 1 length of ribbon 8RW (see chart above). Follow the assembly directions for the posy. Do not cut the thread.

2. Stitch through the middle of the flower at the seam; wrap the thread around the selvage edge to create 2 lobes. Anchor knot the thread into the raw edges; cut the thread.

Wrap thread.

3. Center: Cut 1 length of ribbon 4RW (see chart above). Follow the directions for the half U-gather petal. Tackstitch the raw edges of the center to the raw edges of the flower.

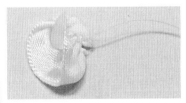

Finished flower

Orchid

Orchid and Majestic Leaf–L (page 131). Use ribbon ⅛″ narrower for leaf than for flower.

SKILL LEVEL: *Advanced* ●●●

Suggested Ribbon

2 different colors of woven or French wire ribbon with medium hand, single- or double-sided

Amount needed:

■ **Center petal:** Approximately 2 × width of Color 1 ribbon, plus ½″ *

■ **Middle and outer petals:** Approximately 15 × width of Color 2 ribbon, plus 1″ *

DIRECTIONS

See General Instructions (page 28) and U-Gather Petals (page 43).

1. Center petal: Measure, pin, and gather stitch 1 U-gather petal 2RW (see chart below). Overlap the raw edges and pull the gathers. Tackstitch through the raw edges; anchor knot and cut the thread.

2. Middle petals: Measure, pin, and gather stitch 2 U-gather petals 3RW (see chart below). Stitch through the selvage edge next to the beginning anchor knot.

3. Gently pull the thread to form the petals over the raw edges of the center petal. Tackstitch through the raw edges; anchor knot and cut the thread.

4. Outer petals: Measure, pin, and gather stitch 3 U-gather petals 3RW (see chart below left). Follow the remaining directions for the middle petals.

Finished flower

Measure

Ribbon width	Center petal: Measure 2RW.*	Middle and outer petals: Measure 3RW per petal.*
1″	2″	3″
⅞″	1¾″	2⅝″
¾″	1½″	2¼″
⅝″	1¼″	1⅞″
½″	1″	1½″
⅜″	¾″	1⅛″

* Do not cut the ribbon until instructed to do so.

Persian Violet

Persian Violet and Spanish Leaf-M (page 128). Use ribbon ⅜″ wider for leaf than for petals.

SKILL LEVEL: *Intermediate*

Suggested Ribbon

Woven or French wire ribbon with medium hand, single- or double-sided

Amount needed:

- 21 × width of project ribbon

DIRECTIONS

See General Instructions (page 28), Shutterbug Button (page 144), and Shutterbug Petals (page 44).

1. Center: Cut 3 lengths of ribbon 2RW (see chart below). Follow the directions for the shutterbug button; cut the thread.

2. Petals: Cut 5 lengths of ribbon 3RW (see chart below). Follow the pinning and gather-stitch directions for the shutterbug petals.

3. Gently pull the thread to form the middle of the flower. Tackstitch through the raw edges.

4. Place the center in the middle of the flower. Tackstitch each overlapped section of the center into the middle of the flower. Anchor knot the thread through the raw edges.

Finished flower

Measure and Cut

Ribbon width	Center: Cut 3 lengths 2RW.	Petals: Cut 5 lengths 3RW.
1″	2″	3″
⅞″	1¾″	2⅝″
¾″	1½″	2¼″
⅝″	1¼″	1⅞″
½″	1″	1½″
⅜″	¾″	1⅛″
¼″	½″	¾″

Fuchsia

Fuchsia and Elizabethan Leaf–L (page 125). Use same ribbon width for both outer flower petals and leaf.

SKILL LEVEL: *Advanced* ●●●

Suggested Ribbon

2 different widths and 3 colors of woven ribbon with soft or medium hand, single- or double-sided

Amount needed:

- **Inner petals:** 12 × width of Color 1 ribbon (Use ⅛" narrower ribbon than for outer petals and bud cap.)

- **Outer petals:** 12 × width of Color 2 ribbon

- **Bud cap:** 3 × width of Color 3 ribbon

Additional Supplies

- 2 folded stamens
- Second threaded needle

Measure and Cut

Inner petals		Outer petals		Bud cap	
Ribbon width	Cut 4 lengths 3RW.	Ribbon width	Cut 4 lengths 3RW.	Ribbon width	Cut 1 length 3RW.
1"	3"	1⅛"	3⅜"	1⅛"	3⅜"
⅞"	2⅝"	1"	3"	1"	3"
¾"	2¼"	⅞"	2⅝"	⅞"	2⅝"
⅝"	1⅞"	¾"	2¼"	¾"	2¼"
½"	1½"	⅝"	1⅞"	⅝"	1⅞"
⅜"	1⅛"	½"	1½"	½"	1½"

DIRECTIONS

See General Instructions (page 28), Shutterbug Petals (page 44), and Bud Cap (page 136).

1. Inner petals: Cut 4 lengths of ribbon 3RW (see chart above). Follow the pinning and gather-stitch directions for shutterbug petals. Gently pull the thread to form the petals; insert the stamens into the middle of the flower. Follow the remaining shutterbug petals directions; cut the thread.

2. Outer petals: Cut 4 lengths of ribbon 3RW (see chart above). Follow the directions for the inner petals. Insert the inner petals into the middle of the flower. Follow the remaining shutterbug petals directions; do not cut the thread.

3. Bud cap: Cut 1 length of ribbon 3RW (see chart above). Using the second needle, follow the directions for the bud cap through the outer gather stitching.

4. Insert the outer petals needle through the center of the cap; pull the petals into the cap. Follow the remaining directions for the bud cap.

Finished flower

Cosmos

Cosmos and Thin Leaf (page 132).
Use ribbon ¼" narrower for leaf than
for flower.

SKILL LEVEL: *Intermediate*

Suggested Ribbon

2 different colors of woven or
French wire ribbon with medium
hand, single- or double-sided

Amount needed:

- **Center:** 9 × width of Color 1
ribbon

- **Petals:** 40 × width of Color 2
ribbon

DIRECTIONS

*See General Instructions (page 28),
Shutterbug Center (page 144), and
Individual-Petal Flower (page 48).*

1. Center: Cut 3 lengths of
ribbon 3RW (see chart below).
Follow the directions for the shutterbug center; cut the thread.

2. Petals: Cut 8 lengths of ribbon
5RW (see chart below). Work with
one length at a time. Fold the
length in half, overlapping the left
side over the right and matching
the raw edges; insert a pin. Repeat
for each length.

3. Flower: Follow the gather-
stitch directions for the
individual-petal flower. Stitch
through the selvage edge next to
the beginning anchor knot. Gently
pull the thread to form the middle
of the flower.

4. Insert the raw edges of the
center into the middle of the
flower; pull the thread tight to
close the middle of the flower.
Tackstitch into the raw edges and
anchor knot the thread.

Finished flower. *Detail option:*
5 small French knots (page 30)
or beads (page 32)

Measure and Cut

Ribbon width	Center: Cut 3 lengths 3RW.	Petals: Cut 8 lengths 5RW.
1"	3"	5"
⅞"	2⅝"	4⅜"
¾"	2¼"	3¾"
⅝"	1⅞"	3⅛"
½"	1½"	2½"
⅜"	1⅛"	1⅞"

Jasmine

Jasmine and Victorian Leaf-M (page 130). Use same ribbon width for both flower and leaf.

SKILL LEVEL: *Advanced* ●●●

Suggested Ribbon

Woven ribbon with soft or medium hand, double-sided

Amount needed:

- Approximately 26 × width of project ribbon*

Additional Supplies

- 1RW × 12" strip of cardstock

DIRECTIONS

See General Instructions (page 28) and Bias-Loop Petals (page 46).

1. Flower: Measure a length of ribbon 26RW. Insert a pin 3RW in from the raw edge (see chart below). Wrap, fold, and pin 8 bias-loop petals. Measure 1RW, cut off the excess ribbon; follow the gather-stitch directions.

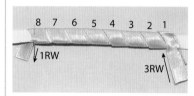

2. Stitch through the selvage edge next to the beginning anchor knot; gently pull the thread to form the middle of the flower.

3. Center: Fold the 3RW length of ribbon (the "tail" from the beginning of the bias-loop petals) in half, with the raw edge to the wrong side. Pull the thread tight to close the middle; anchor knot the thread into the raw edges.

4. Sculpting the center: Tackstitch through the middle of the flower to one selvage edge of the 3RW center at the fold; stitch back down through the middle of the flower.

5. Repeat Step 4 to tackstitch the other selvage edge in place. Anchor knot the thread into the raw edges.

Finished flower. *Detail option:* small French knots (page 30) or beads around outer edge of center (page 32)

Measure

Ribbon width	Measure 1 length 26RW.*	Measure 3RW from raw edge.*
1"	26"	3"
⅞"	22¾"	2⅝"
¾"	19½"	2¼"
⅝"	16¼"	1⅞"
½"	13"	1½"
⅜"	9¾"	1⅛"

Do not cut the ribbon until instructed to do so.

Roses, Queens of the Garden

These are stylized versions of the blooms that so elegantly grow in gardens across the world. Simply stated ... graceful and beautiful.

Most flowers listed in the following chart are accompanied by suggested leaf designs. In some cases, a leaf design is followed by a letter, indicating leaf size:

T = Tiny   **S** = Short   **M** = Medium   **L** = Long   **XL** = Extra-long

For instructions to make the leaves, see Petals and Greenery (page 120).

LINGERIE ROSE ... 109

½" and ⅜" satin ribbons

3 *Simple Leaves*: ⅝" grosgrain ribbon

PRIMROSE ... 114

⅜" grosgrain and ⅝" silk habotai ribbons

Victorian Leaf–M: ⅝" grosgrain ribbon

VICTORIAN ROSE ... 110

⅝" silk bias habotai

3 *Pointed Leaves–S*: 1" silk bias habotai

TEA ROSE ... 115

⅝" silk bias habotai

Rounded Leaf–M: 1" silk bias ribbon

RAMBLIN' ROSE ... 111

⅝" silk bias habotai

Rounded Leaf–S: 1" silk bias ribbon

SHY ROSE ... 116

⅜" satin ribbon

Twin Lazy Loop Leaf–S: ⅝" grosgrain ribbon

VINTAGE ROSE ... 112

⅜" satin ribbon

Twin Elizabethan Leaf–M: ⅜" grosgrain ribbon

FLORIBUNDA ROSE ... 117

½" satin ribbon

Triple Spear-Tip Leaf–M: ⅜" woven ombré ribbon

GYPSY ROSE ... 113

⅜" satin ribbon

Spanish Leaf–S: ⅝" satin ribbon

ELEGANT ROSE ... 118

⅜" satin ribbon

Spanish Leaf–M: ⅝" French wire ribbon

Lingerie Rose

Lingerie Rose with 3 Simple Leaves (page 125). Use ribbon ¼″ wider for leaf than for flower.

SKILL LEVEL: *Intermediate*

Suggested Ribbon

2 different widths and colors of woven ribbon with soft or medium hand, single- or double-sided

Amount needed:

■ **Color 1:** 32 × width of wider ribbon

■ **Color 2:** 32 × width of wider ribbon (Use ⅛″ narrower ribbon for Color 2, in same length as Color 1.)

Additional Supplies

■ 2RW (of wider ribbon) crinoline circle

■ Second threaded needle

Measure and Cut

Width of wider ribbon	Cut 1 length of each color.
1″	32″
⅞″	28″
¾″	24″
⅝″	20″
½″	16″
⅜″	12″
¼″	8″

DIRECTIONS

See General Instructions (page 28), Layering Ribbon (page 16), and Posy (page 38).

1. Cut 1 length of ribbon of each color (see chart above). Follow the directions for layering.

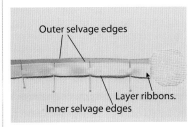

Outer selvage edges
Layer ribbons.
Inner selvage edges

2. Follow the directions for the posy through the gather stitch. Keep the needle threaded, and do not anchor or cut the thread.

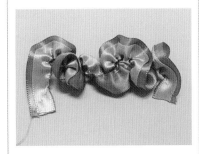

3. Using the second needle, tackstitch the ribbon to the center of the crinoline at the beginning anchor knot.

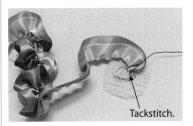

Tackstitch.

4. Gently pull the gathering thread to form the petals. Continuing with the second needle, tackstitch the gathered edges over the raw edges in a spiral around the raw edge of the center. Continue tackstitching the remaining petals in a spiral around and under the previous rows of petals, gathering evenly.

5. Tuck the raw edge of the last petal under the previous row and tackstitch to the crinoline. Anchor knot both threads to the crinoline.

Finished flower

Victorian Rose

Victorian Rose and 3 Pointed Leaves–S (page 138). Use ribbon ⅜" wider for leaf than for flower.

SKILL LEVEL: *Intermediate*

Suggested Ribbon

Silk bias ribbon: habotai, satin, or velvet

Amount needed:

- **Medium-full flower:** 10 × width of project ribbon
- **Full flower:** 12 × width of project ribbon

Additional Supplies

- 2RW crinoline circle
- Second threaded needle

Measure and Cut

Ribbon width	Medium-full flower: Cut 1 length 10RW.	Full flower: Cut 1 length 12RW.
1"	10"	12"
¾"	7½"	9"
⅝"	6¼"	7½"
½"	5"	6"
⁷⁄₁₆"	4⅜"	5¼"

DIRECTIONS

See General Instructions (page 28), Folded-Edge Posy (page 40), and Lingerie Rose (page 109).

1. Cut 1 length of ribbon (see chart above) depending on how full you want the flower. Follow the folding and gather-stitch directions for the folded-edge posy. Keep the needle threaded, and do not anchor or cut the thread.

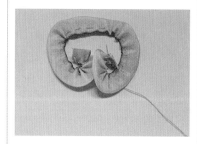

2. Using the second needle, tackstitch the ribbon to the center of the crinoline at the beginning anchor knot.

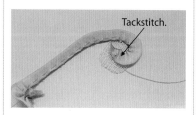

Tackstitch.

3. Follow the remaining assembly directions for the lingerie rose.

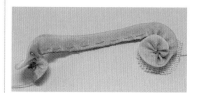

Finished flower. *Detail option:* medium French knot (page 30) or bead (page 32)

Ramblin' Rose

Ramblin' Rose and Rounded Leaf–S (page 137). Use ribbon ⅜″ wider for leaf than for flower.

SKILL LEVEL: *Intermediate* ●●

Suggested Ribbon

2 different colors of silk bias habotai ribbon

Amount needed:

- **Center:** 10 × width of Color 1 ribbon

- **Ruffle:** 18 × width of Color 2 ribbon

Additional Supplies

- 2RW crinoline circle

- Second threaded needle

DIRECTIONS

See General Instructions (page 28), Victorian Rose (page 110), and Double-Edge Rosette (page 36).

1. Center: Cut 1 length of ribbon 10RW (see chart below). Follow the directions for the Victorian rose; cut both threads.

2. Ruffle: Cut 1 length of ribbon 18RW (see chart below). Follow directions for the double-edge rosette through the gather stitching; do not cut the thread.

3. Arrange the ruffle under the center and on top of the crinoline. Gently pull the thread to close the middle of the ruffle.

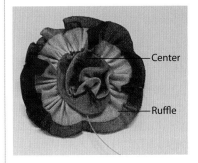

—Center

—Ruffle

4. Tackstitch the center gathers to the crinoline; anchor knot the thread into the crinoline.

Finished flower

Measure and Cut

Ribbon width	Center: Cut 1 length 10RW.	Ruffle: Cut 1 length 18RW.
1″	10″	18″
¾″	7½″	13½″
⅝″	6¼″	11¼″
½″	5″	9″
⁷⁄₁₆″	4⅜″	7⅞″

Vintage Rose

Vintage Rose and Twin Elizabethan Leaf–M (page 134). Use same ribbon width for both flower and leaf.

SKILL LEVEL: *Intermediate* ●●

Suggested Ribbon

Woven ribbon with soft or medium hand, single- or double-sided

Amount needed:

- 50 × width of project ribbon

Additional Supplies

- 3 folded stamens

DIRECTIONS

See General Instructions (page 28), Shutterbug Center (page 144), and Shutterbug Petals (page 44).

1. Inner petals: Cut 3 lengths of ribbon 3RW (see chart below). Follow assembly directions for the shutterbug center; insert the stamens through the opening of the center. Pull the thread tight to close the center; anchor knot and cut the thread.

2. Middle petals: Cut 4 lengths of ribbon 4RW (see chart below). Follow the pinning and gather-stitch directions for the shutterbug petals. Insert the inner petals into the opening of the middle petals; pull the thread tight to close the opening. Tackstitch and anchor knot through the raw edges; cut the thread.

3. Outer petals: Cut 5 lengths of ribbon 5RW (see chart below left). Follow the directions for the middle petals; insert the middle petals into the opening of the outer petals.

4. Pull the thread tightly to close the opening. Tackstitch and anchor knot through the raw edges; cut the thread.

Finished flower

Measure and Cut

Ribbon width	Inner petals: Cut 3 lengths 3RW.	Middle petals: Cut 4 lengths 4RW.	Outer petals: Cut 5 lengths 5RW.
1″	3″	4″	5″
⅞″	2⅝″	3½″	4⅜″
¾″	2¼″	3″	3¾″
⅝″	1⅞″	2½″	3⅛″
½″	1½″	2″	2½″
⅜″	1⅛″	1½″	1⅞″

Gypsy Rose

Gypsy Rose and Spanish Leaf–S (page 128). Use ribbon ¼″ wider for leaf than for flower.

SKILL LEVEL: *Intermediate* ●●

Suggested Ribbon

Woven ribbon with soft or medium hand, single- or double-sided

Amount needed:

- Approximately 60 × width of project ribbon, plus ½″ *

Additional Supplies

- 3RW crinoline circle
- Second threaded needle
- 5 folded stamens

Measure

Ribbon width	Measure 3RW per petal.*
1″	3″
⅞″	2⅝″
¾″	2¼″
⅝″	1⅞″
½″	1½″
⅜″	1⅛″

* Do not cut the ribbon until instructed to do so.

DIRECTIONS

See General Instructions (page 28) and U-Gather Petals (page 43).

1. Measure, pin, and gather stitch 20 U-gather petals 3RW (see chart below left). Gently pull the thread to form the petals. Keep the needle threaded, and do not anchor or cut the thread.

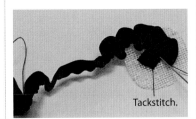

2. Using the second needle, tackstitch the beginning raw edge to the center of the crinoline.

Tackstitch.

3. Poke a small hole in the center of the crinoline; insert the stamens through the opening. Place the raw edge over the opening; using the second needle, tackstitch the stamens in place under the raw edge. Do not anchor or cut the thread.

4. Continuing with the second needle, tackstitch the V-shaped loop of each of the first 5 petals in a spiral around and over the raw edge.

5. Continue tackstitching the remaining petals in a spiral around and under each previous row of petals. Tuck the raw edge of the last petal under the previous row and tackstitch to the crinoline. Anchor knot both threads to the crinoline.

Finished flower

Primrose

Primrose and Victorian Leaf–M (page 130). Use ribbon ¼″ wider for leaf than for flower.

SKILL LEVEL: *Intermediate*

Suggested Ribbon

Woven ribbon for petals and silk bias habotai ribbon for center

Amount needed:

■ **Center:** 4 × width of wider ribbon (Use ¼″ wider ribbon than for inner and outer petals.)

■ **Inner and outer petals:** 33 × width of narrower ribbon

DIRECTIONS

See General Instructions (page 28), Woven and Silk Bias Berries (page 149), and Shutterbug Petals (page 44).

1. Center: Cut 1 length of ribbon 4RW (see chart below). Follow the directions for the stuffed bias berry. Cut the thread.

2. Inner petals: Cut 3 lengths of ribbon 3RW (see chart below). Follow directions for the shutterbug petals through the gather stitching; gently pull the thread to form the petals.

3. Insert the center from the wrong side into the middle of the inner petals. Flip the raw edges of the inner petals over the center. Tackstitch and anchor knot the thread through the raw edges; cut the thread.

4. Outer petals: Cut 8 lengths of ribbon 3RW (see chart below left). Follow directions for the shutterbug petals through the gather stitching. Gently pull the thread to close the opening, with the raw edges just touching. Anchor knot the thread.

5. Place the center and inner petals over the raw edges of the outer petals. Tackstitch each overlapped section of the inner petals to the middle of the flower; anchor knot the thread through the raw edges.

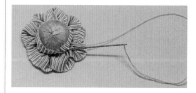

Finished flower. *Detail option:* small French knots (page 30) or beads around outer edge of center (page 32)

Measure and Cut

Center		Inner and outer petals	
Ribbon width	**Cut 1 length 4RW.**	**Ribbon width**	**Inner petals:** Cut 3 lengths 3RW. **Outer petals:** Cut 8 lengths 3RW.
1″	4″	¾″	2¼″
¾″	3″	½″	1½″
⅝″	2½″	⅜″	1⅛″

Tea Rose

Tea Rose and Rounded Leaf–M (page 137). Use ribbon ⅜" wider for leaf than for flower.

SKILL LEVEL: *Advanced* ●●●

Suggested Ribbon

Silk bias ribbon: habotai, satin, or velvet

Amount needed:

■ Approximately 24 × width of project ribbon, plus ½" *

Additional Supplies

■ 2RW crinoline circle

Measure

Ribbon width	Measure 2RW per petal.*
1"	2"
¾"	1½"
⅝"	1¼"
½"	1"
⁷⁄₁₆"	⅞"

* Do not cut the ribbon until instructed to do so.

DIRECTIONS

See General Instructions (page 28), U-Gather Petals (page 43), and Triple Delight (page 61). Where the directions for U-gather petals refer to the outer selvage edge, that will be the folded edge in this flower; the U-gather inner selvage edge will be the bias edge in this flower.

1. Fold and gently finger-press the width of the ribbon in half. Pin 12 U-gather petals 2RW (see chart below left).

First row: Gather stitch 1 petal.

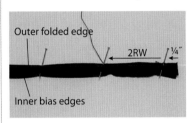

Outer folded edge
2RW
¼"
Inner bias edges

2. Place the raw edge in the center of the crinoline. Loop the thread over the entire width of the ribbon; stitch into the crinoline to secure the gathered edge of the first individual petal. Pull the thread tight and anchor knot.

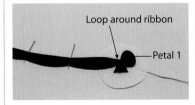

Loop around ribbon
Petal 1

3. Gather stitch and secure the gathered edges of each of the next 2 individual petals.

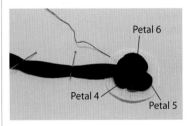

Petal 3
Petal 1
Petal 2

4. Second row: Gather stitch 3 more individual petals.

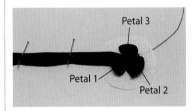

Petal 6
Petal 4
Petal 5

5. Third row: Gather stitch the remaining 6 petals in 1 length. Tackstitch the gathered edges in a spiral around the previous row. Tackstitch the raw edge of the last petal under the last row of petals; anchor the thread.

11 10
12
9
8
Petal 7

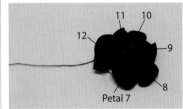

Finished flower. *Detail option:* medium French knot (page 30) or bead (page 32)

Shy Rose

Shy Rose and Twin Lazy Loop Leaf–S (page 134). Use ribbon ¼″ wider for leaf than for flower.

SKILL LEVEL: *Advanced*

Suggested Ribbon

Woven ribbon with soft or medium hand, single- or double-sided

Amount needed:

- 77½ × width of project ribbon

Additional Supplies

- 2RW × 8″ strip of cardstock
- 2RW crinoline circle
- 5 folded stamens

DIRECTIONS

See General Instructions (page 28) and Spiral-Loop Petals (page 45).

1. Outer petals: Cut 1 length of ribbon 44RW (see chart below). Follow the gather-stitch and seaming directions for the spiral-loop petal, evenly and loosely looping the ribbon 8 times over the cardstock.

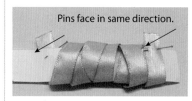

Pins face in same direction.

2. Gently pull the thread to fit the petals just inside the crinoline circle. Tackstitch the seam to the crinoline. Tackstitch the last petal flat. Overlap the next petal and tackstitch this flat. Repeat this step for each remaining petal.

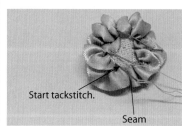

Start tackstitch.

Seam

3. Poke a small hole in the center of the crinoline; insert the stamens through the opening; tackstitch to the wrong side of the crinoline.

4. Inner petals: Cut 1 length of ribbon 33½RW (see chart below left). Follow the directions for the outer petals (Step 1), loosely looping the ribbon 6 times over the cardstock.

5. Place the inner petals onto the crinoline inside the outer petals, inserting the stamens through the opening of the inner petals. Tackstitch the inner loop of each petal to the crinoline. Anchor knot the thread.

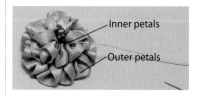

Inner petals

Outer petals

Finished flower

Measure and Cut

Ribbon width	Outer petals: Cut 1 length 44RW.	Inner petals: Cut 1 length 33½RW.
1″	44″	33½″
⅞″	38½″	29⁵⁄₁₆″
¾″	33″	25⅛″
⅝″	27½″	20¹⁵⁄₁₆″
½″	22″	16¾″
⅜″	16½″	12⁹⁄₁₆″

Floribunda Rose

Floribunda Rose and Triple Spear-Tip Leaf–M (page 132). Use ribbon ⅛″ narrower for leaf than for flower.

SKILL LEVEL: *Intermediate* 🌢🌢

Suggested Ribbon

3 different colors of woven ribbon with soft or medium hand, double-sided

Amount needed:

- **Inner petals:** Approximately 11 × width of Color 1 ribbon*
- **Middle petals:** Approximately 14 × width of Color 2 ribbon*
- **Outer petals:** Approximately 35 × width of Color 3 ribbon*

Additional Supplies

- 4 folded stamens

Measure

Ribbon width	Inner petals: Measure 3RW per petal.*	Middle petals: Measure 4RW per petal.*	Outer petals: Measure 5RW per petal.*
1″	3″	4″	5″
⅞″	2⅝″	3½″	4⅜″
¾″	2¼″	3″	3¾″
⅝″	1⅞″	2½″	3⅛″
½″	1½″	2″	2½″
⅜″	1⅛″	1½″	1⅞″

* Do not cut the ribbon until instructed to do so.

DIRECTIONS

See General Instructions (page 28) and Veronica (page 72).

1. For each layer of petals, follow the directions for Veronica.

Inner petals: Measure, pin, and gather stitch 3 folded petals 3RW (see chart above). Insert the stamens into the center; pull the thread tight to close the middle. Anchor knot and cut off the thread.

2. Middle petals: Measure, pin, and gather stitch 3 folded petals 4RW (see chart above). Gently pull the thread to form the petals.

3. Insert the inner petals into the opening; pull the thread tight to close the middle. Anchor knot and cut off the thread.

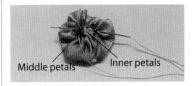

Middle petals   Inner petals

4. Outer petals: Measure, pin, and gather stitch 6 folded petals 5RW (see chart at left). Gently pull the thread to form the petals.

5. Insert the middle and inner petals into the opening; pull the thread tight to close the middle. Anchor knot and cut off the thread.

Finished flower

Elegant Rose

Elegant Rose and Spanish Leaf–M (page 128). Use ribbon ¼" wider for leaf than for flower petals.

SKILL LEVEL: *Intermediate*

Suggested Ribbon

Woven ribbon with soft or medium hand, single- or double-sided

Amount needed:

- Approximately 93 × width of project ribbon, plus ½" *

Additional Supplies

- 4RW crinoline circle
- Second threaded needle

DIRECTIONS

See General Instructions (page 28) and Ruched Petals (page 47).

1. Inner petals: Insert a pin ¼" from the raw edge. Measure, pin, and gather stitch 6 ruched petals 2RW (see chart below). Do not measure ¼" from the last petal or cut the ribbon. Gently pull the thread to form the petals. Keep the needle threaded, and do not anchor or cut the thread. Use the second needle to tackstitch the beginning raw edge to the crinoline.

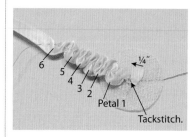

2. Still using the second needle, tackstitch the center of each remaining petal in a spiral around the first petal, covering the raw edge.

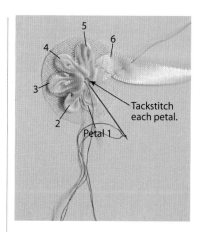

3. Middle petals: Beginning at the end of the last petal of the inner petal row, measure, pin, and gather stitch the next 12 petals 3RW (see chart below left) with the first needle.

4. With the second needle, tackstitch the center of each petal in a spiral around and under the previous row of petals.

Measure

Ribbon width	Inner petals: Measure 2RW per petal.*	Middle and outer petals: Measure 3RW per petal.*
1"	2"	3"
⅞"	1¾"	2⅝"
¾"	1½"	2¼"
⅝"	1¼"	1⅞"
½"	1"	1½"
⅜"	¾"	1⅛"

* Do not cut the ribbon until instructed to do so.

5. Outer petals: Beginning at the end of the last petal of the middle petal row, measure, pin, and gather stitch the next 15 petals 3RW (see chart on previous page) with the first needle. Measure ¼" from the last petal, and cut off the ribbon.

6. Follow the directions in Step 4 to tackstitch the outer petals in place. Trim the crinoline. Tackstitch the raw edges of the last petal to the back of the crinoline. Anchor knot both threads to the crinoline.

Tackstitch.

Finished flower

Elegant Rose Hat Ornament, 5½" × 3½"

Black and Pink Rose Bracelet, ⅞" × 7½"

Ribbon Umbrella, 2¼" × 6¼"; Shy Rose Corsage, 2¾" × 3½"; Ramblin' Rose Corsage, 3" × 3½"

Petals and Greenery

Each flower listed in the garden chapters has been paired with a leaf to complete the design. You will find the leaves in this chapter. The first section lists designs that can be used for a leaf, an individual petal, or a bud; the second section lists designs that are specifically made to be leaves.

Leaves, Individual Petals, or Buds

The following designs can be made into a leaf, petal, or bud; the only difference is the color of ribbon you choose to make the design from. Any of these petals can be turned into a flower using the individual-petal flower design (page 48).

Couture Leaf, Petal, or Bud; and Knot Center ... 122

Lazy Loop Leaf, Petal, or Bud ... 122

Parisian Leaf, Petal, or Bud ... 123

Pinwheel Leaf, Petal, or Bud ... 123

Kimono Leaf, Petal, or Bud ... 124

Triangle-Fold Leaf, Petal, or Bud ... 124

Elizabethan Leaf, Petal, or Bud ... 125

Simple Leaf, Petal, or Bud ... 125

Spear-Tip Leaf, Petal, or Bud ... 126

Greenery

The following leaf designs have unique shapes or qualities that make them suitable for one flower or another. A few are made specifically for the flowers they are named for.

Lollypop Leaf ... 126

Fleur-de-Lis Leaf ... 127

Lance Leaf ... 127

Spanish Leaf ... 128

Arrowhead Leaf ... 128

Teardrop Leaf ... 129

 Edwardian Leaf ... 129

 Victorian Leaf ... 130

 Jester's Leaf ... 130

 Iris Leaf ... 131

 Majestic Leaf ... 131

 Thin Leaf ... 132

 Triple Spear-Tip Leaf ... 132

 Crown Leaf ... 133

 Twin Elizabethan Leaf ... 134

 Twin Lazy Loop Leaf ... 134

 Regal Leaf ... 135

 Kimono Calyx and Bud ... 135

 Bud Cap ... 136

 Simple Calyx ... 136

 Morning Glory Leaf ... 137

 Rounded Leaf ... 137

 Double-Edge Leaf ... 138

 Pointed Leaf ... 138

GENERAL ASSEMBLY DIRECTIONS
(LEAF, PETAL, OR BUD)

See General Instructions (page 28).

1. Follow the directions to fold, cut, loop, pin, or knot the ribbon.

2. Anchor knot the thread into the selvage edge ⅛" up from the raw edge.

3. Gather stitch across the raw edges.

4. Tackstitch through the raw edges and anchor knot the thread.

Ribbon Measurement

Each set of directions will give an RW measurement for the design; use the Ribbon Cutting Chart (page 17) to find the correct measurement for the ribbon width you are using.

Couture Leaf, Petal, or Bud; and Knot Center

Couture Knot Leaf, Petal/Bud, and Knot Center

SKILL LEVEL: *Easy* ●

Suggested Ribbon

Woven or French wire ribbon with soft or medium hand, double-sided

Ribbon Measurement

- Leaf or petal/bud: 8RW

- Knot center: 6RW

See the Ribbon Cutting Chart (page 17).

DIRECTIONS

See General Assembly Directions (page 121).

1. Leaf or petal/bud: Cut 1 length of ribbon 8RW. Tie an overhand knot into the middle of the length. Use bent-nose tweezers to pull the raw edges through the opening. Pull the knot tight.

2. Stitch across both halves of ribbon.

Finished leaf or petal/bud.

3. Knot Center: Cut 1 length of ribbon 6RW. Repeat Step 1.

Finished knot center

🌼 *tip*

For a shorter length, it is easier to tie the knot, and then cut the ribbon.

Lazy Loop Leaf, Petal, or Bud

Group of Lazy Loop Leaves

SKILL LEVEL: *Easy* ●

Suggested Ribbon

Woven or French wire ribbon with soft or medium hand, double-sided

Ribbon Measurement

- **Tiny:** 6RW

- **Short:** 8RW

- **Medium:** 10RW

- **Long:** 12RW

- **X-Long:** 14RW

See the Ribbon Cutting Chart (page 17).

DIRECTIONS

See General Assembly Directions (page 121).

1. Cut 1 length of ribbon. Fold the length of ribbon in half; overlap the left raw edge over the right and pin the raw edges.

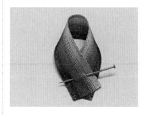

2. Stitch across both halves of ribbon.

Finished leaf or petal/bud

Parisian Leaf, Petal, or Bud

Parisian Leaf and Petal/Bud

SKILL LEVEL: *Intermediate* 🌢🌢

Suggested Ribbon

Woven or French wire ribbon with soft or medium hand, single- or double-sided

Ribbon Measurement

- Short: 8RW

- Medium: 10RW

See the Ribbon Cutting Chart (page 17).

DIRECTIONS

See General Instructions (page 28) and Knot Center (page 122).

1. Cut 1 length of ribbon. Tie an overhand knot into the middle of the length. Fold the length in half, right side in; insert a pin ½RW into the raw edges. Insert a pin into the selvage edges 1RW from the raw edge for a petal/bud or 2RW for a leaf.

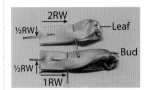

2. Anchor knot the thread at the selvage edge next to the pin. Using assembly stitch 1, stitch diagonally toward where the pin meets the raw edges. Open the leaf flat.

Finished leaf and petal/bud

Pinwheel Leaf, Petal, or Bud

Pinwheel Leaf and Petal/Bud

SKILL LEVEL: *Intermediate* 🌢🌢

Suggested Ribbon

Woven or French wire ribbon with soft or medium hand, double-sided

Ribbon Measurement

- 4RW

See the Ribbon Cutting Chart (page 17).

DIRECTIONS

See General Assembly Directions (page 121).

1. Cut 1 length of ribbon 4RW. Fold the length of ribbon in half to find the center. Fold the left side forward at a 90° angle. Fold the right side back and over, and then forward over the left side. Overlap the right raw edge over the left. Insert a pin through both layers of ribbon.

2. Stitch across and through both layers of ribbon.

Finished leaf or petal/bud

Kimono Leaf, Petal, or Bud

Kimono Leaf and Petal/Bud

SKILL LEVEL: *Intermediate* ● ●

Suggested Ribbon

Woven or French wire ribbon with soft or medium hand, single- or double-sided

Ribbon Measurement

- 3RW

See the Ribbon Cutting Chart (page 17).

DIRECTIONS

See General Assembly Directions (page 121).

1. Cut 1 length of ribbon 3RW. Fold the length of ribbon in half to find the center. Fold the left side down and at an angle, with the raw

edges below the selvage edge. Fold and overlap the right side over the left. Insert a pin through all the layers of ribbon.

2. Stitch across and through all of the layers of ribbon.

Finished leaf or petal/bud

Triangle-Fold Leaf, Petal, or Bud

Triangle-Fold Leaf and Petal/Bud

SKILL LEVEL: *Easy* ●

Suggested Ribbon

Woven or French wire ribbon with soft or medium hand, single- or double-sided

Ribbon Measurement

- 2RW

See the Ribbon Cutting Chart (page 17).

DIRECTIONS

See General Assembly Directions (page 121).

1. Cut 1 length of ribbon 2RW. Fold the length of ribbon in half to find the center. Fold

each side down at an angle and even with the raw edges. Insert a pin through all the layers of ribbon.

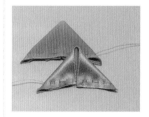

2. Stitch across and through all the layers of ribbon.

Finished leaf or petal/bud

Elizabethan Leaf, Petal, or Bud

Group of Elizabethan Leaves

SKILL LEVEL: *Intermediate* ● ●

Suggested Ribbon

Woven or French wire with soft or medium hand, single- or double-sided

Ribbon Measurement

- **Short:** 4RW
- **Medium:** 6RW
- **Long:** 8RW

See the Ribbon Cutting Chart (page 17).

DIRECTIONS

See General Assembly Directions (page 121).

1. Cut 1 length of ribbon. Fold the ribbon length in half, right side in; match the raw edges.

2. Anchor knot the thread into the selvage edges at the fold. Stitch the selvage edges together with assembly stitch 1; anchor knot the thread.

3. Open the leaf; gently poke the tip out with a stuffing tool. Stitch across both halves of ribbon.

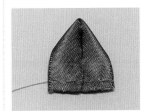

Finished leaf or petal/bud

Simple Leaf, Petal, or Bud

Simple Leaf and Petal/Bud

SKILL LEVEL: *Easy* ●

Suggested Ribbon

Woven, French wire, or silk bias ribbon with soft or medium hand, single- or double-sided

Ribbon Measurement

- 2RW

See the Ribbon Cutting Chart (page 17).

DIRECTIONS

See General Assembly Directions (page 121) and Elizabethan Leaf, Petal, or Bud (at left).

1. Cut 1 length of ribbon 2RW. Fold the ribbon length in half, right side in; match the raw edges.

2. Follow the seam directions for the Elizabethan leaf, petal, or bud.

3. Open the leaf; gently poke the tip out with a stuffing tool. Stitch across and through all of the layers of ribbon.

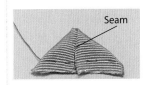

Seam

Finished leaf or petal/bud

Spear-Tip Leaf, Petal, or Bud

Group of Spear-Tip Leaves

SKILL LEVEL: *Advanced*

Suggested Ribbon

Woven or French wire with soft or medium hand, single- or double-sided

Ribbon Measurement

- **Short:** 4RW
- **Medium:** 6RW
- **Long:** 8RW

See the Ribbon Cutting Chart (page 17).

DIRECTIONS

See General Instructions (page 28).

1. Cut 1 length of ribbon. Fold the ribbon length in half, wrong side in; match the raw edges. Fold the width of the ribbon in half. Insert a pin through the fold 1RW from the raw edges.

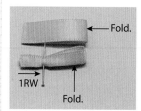

2. Anchor knot the thread into the selvage edges at the raw edges. Using assembly stitch 1, stitch diagonally toward where the pin meets the fold. Anchor knot the thread.

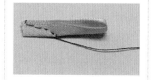

3. Open and unfold the ribbon to expose the loop of the ribbon. Insert the needle through the 2 layers of ribbon to the center of the top fold.

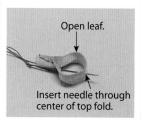

Open leaf.

Insert needle through center of top fold.

4. Stitch through the fold at the right selvage edge (A) and then through the fold at the left selvage edge (B). Pull the thread to form the point (C). Tackstitch and anchor knot the thread.

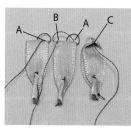

A B A C

Finished leaf or petal/bud

Lollypop Leaf

Lollypop Leaf

SKILL LEVEL: *Easy* ◉

Suggested Ribbon

Woven ribbon with soft, medium, or stiff hand, single- or double-sided

Ribbon Measurement

- **Soft hand:** 6RW
- **Medium hand:** 7RW
- **Stiff hand:** 8RW

See the Ribbon Cutting Chart (page 17).

DIRECTIONS

See General Instructions (page 28) and Posy (page 38).

Cut 1 length of ribbon according to the hand of the project ribbon. Follow the directions for the posy.

Finished leaf

Fleur-de-Lis Leaf

Fleur-de-Lis Leaf

SKILL LEVEL: *Intermediate* ●●

Suggested Ribbon

Woven or French wire ribbon with soft or medium hand, double-sided

Ribbon Measurement

▪ 9RW

See the Ribbon Cutting Chart (page 17).

DIRECTIONS

See General Instructions (page 28) and Folded Petals (page 41).

1. Measure and pin a folded-petal flower, 2RW, 3RW, and 2RW, with the folds facing inward.

2. Fold the ribbon in half, right side in; match the raw edges, taking care to match outer selvage edges as well. Use assembly stitch 2 to stitch with a ⅛" seam allowance, being sure to end stitch at the inner selvage edge. Anchor knot the thread into the raw edges at the inner selvage edge.

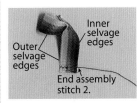

3. Stitch into the inner selvage edge next to the seam; gather stitch along the selvage edge, the folds, and the remaining selvage edges; loop over the edges.

4. Gently pull the thread to form the lobes of the leaf; anchor knot the thread into the raw edges.

Finished leaf

Lance Leaf

Lance Leaf

SKILL LEVEL: *Advanced* ●●●

Suggested Ribbon

Woven or French wire ribbon with soft or medium hand, single- or double-sided

Ribbon Measurement

▪ 5RW

See the Ribbon Cutting Chart (page 17).

DIRECTIONS

See General Assembly Directions (page 121).

1. Cut 1 length of ribbon 5RW. Fold the ribbon length in half, right side in; match the raw edges. Insert a pin 1RW from the fold. Fold the ribbon at a 90° angle to the pin and re-pin to hold.

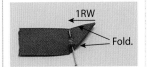

2. Using assembly stitch 2, stitch through the fold. Anchor knot the thread. Using assembly stitch 1, stitch the shortened selvage edges together.

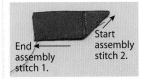

3. Open the leaf. Stitch across both layers of ribbon.

Finished leaf

Spanish Leaf

Group of Spanish Leaves

SKILL LEVEL: *Advanced* ●●●

Suggested Ribbon

Woven or French wire ribbon with soft or medium hand, single- or double-sided

Ribbon Measurement

- Short: 6RW
- Medium: 8RW
- Long: 10RW

See the Ribbon Cutting Chart (page 17).

DIRECTIONS:

See General Assembly Directions (page 121) and Lance Leaf (page 127).

1. Cut 1 length of ribbon. Fold the ribbon length in half, right side in; match the raw edges.

Follow the directions of the lance leaf to stitch assembly stitch 2; anchor knot the thread.

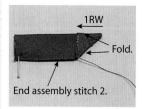

End assembly stitch 2.

2. Gather stitch the shortened selvage edges together. Gently pull in the gathers to form the leaf. Tackstitch and anchor knot the thread into the selvage edges. Follow the remaining directions for the lance leaf.

Finished leaf

Arrowhead Leaf

Arrowhead Leaf

SKILL LEVEL: *Advanced* ●●●

Suggested Ribbon

Woven or French wire ribbon with soft or medium hand, single- or double-sided

Ribbon Measurement

- 6RW

See the Ribbon Cutting Chart (page 17).

DIRECTIONS

See General Assembly Directions (page 121) and Lance Leaf (page 127).

1. Cut 1 length of ribbon 6RW. Follow the directions for the lance leaf. Do not cut the thread.

2. Gather, tackstitch, and anchor knot the thread. Fold a tuck into the middle of the length of the leaf, right side in, about ½RW wide. Tackstitch the tuck at the seam; anchor knot the thread.

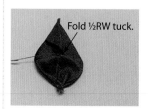

Fold ½RW tuck.

Finished leaf

Teardrop Leaf

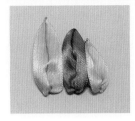

Group of Teardrop Leaves

SKILL LEVEL: *Advanced* ●●●

Suggested Ribbon

Woven or French wire ribbon with soft or medium hand, single- or double-sided

Ribbon Measurement

- Short: 7RW
- Medium: 9RW
- Long: 11RW

See the Ribbon Cutting Chart (page 17).

DIRECTIONS

See General Assembly Directions (page 121) and Lance Leaf (page 127).

1. Cut 1 length of ribbon. Follow the directions for pinning the tip of the lance leaf. Insert a pin into the selvage edge 1RW from the raw edges.

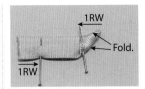

2. Follow the lance leaf directions to stitch the tip. Using assembly stitch 1, stitch the shortened selvage edges together up to the pin. Anchor knot the thread.

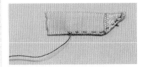

3. Gather stitch diagonally toward the point on the outer selvage edge that is ⅛" in from the raw edges. Pull the thread to gather the ribbon; tackstitch and anchor knot the thread into the raw edges.

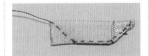

Finished leaf

Edwardian Leaf

Group of Edwardian Leaves

SKILL LEVEL: *Easy* ●

Suggested Ribbon

Woven or French wire ribbon with soft or medium hand, single- or double-sided

Ribbon Measurement

- Short: 4RW
- Medium: 6RW
- Long: 8RW

See the Ribbon Cutting Chart (page 17).

DIRECTIONS

See General Assembly Directions (page 121).

1. Cut 1 length of ribbon. Fold the ribbon length in half, right side in; match the raw edges. Anchor knot the thread into the selvage edges at the fold.

2. Gather stitch the selvage edges together. Gently pull the thread to form the leaf. Tackstitch and anchor knot the thread.

3. Open the leaf. Stitch across both halves of the ribbon.

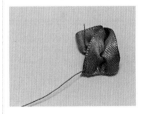

Finished leaf

Victorian Leaf

Group of Victorian Leaves

SKILL LEVEL: *Easy* 🌢

Suggested Ribbon

Woven or French wire ribbon with soft or medium hand, single- or double-sided

Ribbon Measurement

▪ **Short:** 6RW

▪ **Medium:** 8RW

▪ **Long:** 10RW

See the Ribbon Cutting Chart (page 17).

DIRECTIONS

See General Assembly Directions (page 121).

1. Cut 1 length of ribbon. Fold the ribbon length in half, right side in; match the raw edges. Using assembly stitch 2, stitch the raw edges together with a ⅛″ seam allowance. Anchor knot the thread into the raw edges.

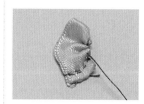

2. Gather stitch through the selvage edges to the fold. Gently pull in the gathers to form the leaf. Tackstitch and anchor knot the thread into the selvage edges.

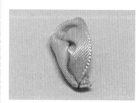

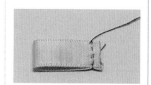

Finished leaf

Jester's Leaf

Jester's Leaf

SKILL LEVEL: *Intermediate* 🌢🌢

Suggested Ribbon

Woven or French wire ribbon with soft or medium hand, double-sided

Ribbon Measurement

▪ 8RW

See the Ribbon Cutting Chart (page 17).

DIRECTIONS

See General Instructions (page 28) and Fleur-de-Lis Leaf (page 127).

1. Cut 1 length of ribbon 8RW. Measure 3RW and fold the ribbon forward at a 90° angle; fold the ribbon again in the same direction. Measure 3RW from the last fold.

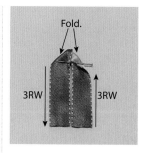

Fold.

3RW   3RW

2. Follow the seam and gather-stitching directions for the fleur-de-lis leaf.

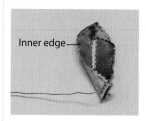

Inner edge

3. Gently pull the thread to form the lobes of the leaf; anchor knot the thread into the raw edges.

Finished leaf

Iris Leaf

Iris Leaf

Suggested Ribbon

Woven or French wire ribbon with soft or medium hand, single- or double-sided

Ribbon Measurement

- 10RW

See the Ribbon Cutting Chart (page 17).

DIRECTIONS

See General Instructions (page 28) and Knot Center (page 122).

1. Cut 1 length of ribbon 10RW. Tie an overhand knot into the length, just shy of the middle. Fold the ribbon length in half, wrong side in. Fold the raw edges up ⅛".

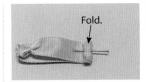

Fold.

2. Fold the width of the ribbon in half. Insert a pin into the selvage edges 1RW from the folded end. Anchor knot the thread into the selvage edges at the folded raw edges.

1RW

Fold.

3. Whipstitch through the selvage edges to the pin. Anchor knot the thread.

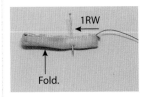

Finished leaf

Majestic Leaf

Group of Majestic Leaves

Suggested Ribbon

Woven or French wire ribbon with soft or medium hand, double-sided

Ribbon Measurement

- **Short:** 4RW
- **Medium:** 6RW
- **Long:** 8RW

See the Ribbon Cutting Chart (page 17).

DIRECTIONS

See General Instructions (page 28) and Elizabethan Leaf, Petal, or Bud (page 125).

1. Cut 1 length of ribbon. Fold and gently finger-press the width of the ribbon to two-thirds the original width.

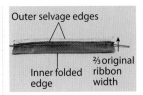

Outer selvage edges

Inner folded edge

⅔ original ribbon width

2. Fold the ribbon length in half, folded side in; match the raw edges. Follow the remaining directions for the Elizabethan leaf from Step 2, using a gather stitch along the inner folded edges.

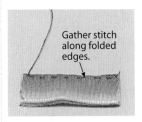

Gather stitch along folded edges.

Finished leaf

Thin Leaf

Thin Leaf

SKILL LEVEL: *Easy* 🌢

Suggested Ribbon

Woven or French wire ribbon with soft or medium hand, double-sided

Ribbon Measurement

■ 64RW

See the Ribbon Cutting Chart (page 17).

DIRECTIONS

See General Instructions (page 28).

1. Cut a length of ribbon 64RW. Measure 20RW in from the raw edge; insert a pin into the ribbon. Fold the length in half and tackstitch the raw edge to the wrong side of the ribbon to form the first lobe.

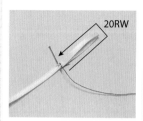

2. Repeat Step 1 to make 2 more lobes; tackstitch the ribbon to the wrong side of the first lobe each time.

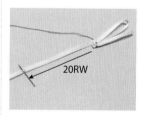

Finished leaf

Triple Spear-Tip Leaf

Group of Triple Spear-Tip Leaves

SKILL LEVEL: *Advanced* 🌢🌢🌢

Suggested Ribbon

Woven or French wire ribbon with soft or medium hand, single- or double-sided

Ribbon Measurement

■ **Short:** 6RW

■ **Medium:** 8RW

■ **Long:** 10RW

See the Ribbon Cutting Chart (page 17).

DIRECTIONS

See General Instructions (page 28) and Spear-Tip Leaf, Petal, or Bud (page 126).

1. Cut 3 lengths of ribbon the same size, or make 1 of them longer.

Follow the directions for the spear-tip leaf for each length.

2. Tackstitch through the raw edges of all the leaves. Anchor knot the thread.

Finished leaf

Crown Leaf

Crown Leaf

SKILL LEVEL: *Advanced* ◕◕◕

Suggested Ribbon

Woven or French wire ribbon with soft or medium hand, single- or double-sided

Ribbon Measurement

- 14RW

See the Ribbon Cutting Chart (page 17).

DIRECTIONS

See General Instructions (page 28) and Kimono Leaf, Petal, or Bud (page 124).

1. Cut 1 length of ribbon 14RW.

Center lobe: Fold the length in half to find the center. Fold and pin the ribbon as given in Step 1 of Kimono Leaf, Petal or Bud (page 124).

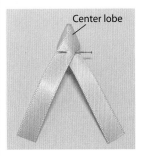

Center lobe

2. Right-hand lobe: Work with the first lobe's point facing you. Hold onto the right-hand raw edge and tuck it under, right side up, against the wrong side of the left-hand edge of this lobe; this will form a pointed lobe. Insert a pin through the layers.

Left-hand lobe: Hold onto the left-hand raw edge and tuck it under, right side up, against the wrong side of the right-hand edge of this lobe. Insert a pin through the layers.

Tuck under.   Tuck under.

3. Anchor knot the thread into the selvage edge of the lobe on the right. Gather stitch across each lobe, through all the layers of ribbon, back to the selvage edge of the lobe on the left.

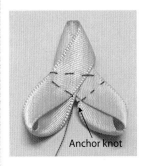
Anchor knot

4. Gently pull the thread to form the middle of the leaf. Tackstitch and anchor knot the thread into the raw edges.

Finished leaf

Twin Elizabethan Leaf

Group of Twin
Elizabethan Leaves

SKILL LEVEL: *Intermediate* 🌢🌢

Suggested Ribbon

Woven or French wire
ribbon with soft or
medium hand, single-
or double-sided

Ribbon Measurement

- **Short:** 10RW

- **Medium:** 12RW

- **Long:** 14RW

*See the Ribbon Cutting
Chart (page 17).*

DIRECTIONS

*See General Instructions
(page 28).*

1. Cut 1 length of
ribbon. Fold the ribbon
length in half, right side
in; match the raw edges.

Using assembly stitch 2,
stitch the raw edges
together with a ⅛" seam
allowance. Anchor knot
the thread into the raw
edges; cut the thread.

2. Fold the length
so that the seam is in
the middle of the loop.
Match the selvage edges;
anchor knot the thread
at the fold. Use assembly
stitch 1 to stitch the
selvage edges together;
anchor knot and cut the
thread.

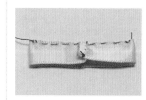

3. Open the leaf; gently
poke the tips out with a
stuffing tool.

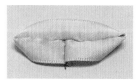

Finished leaf

Twin Lazy Loop Leaf

Group of Twin
Lazy Loop Leaves

SKILL LEVEL: *Easy* 🌢

Suggested Ribbon

Woven or French
wire ribbon with soft
or medium hand,
single- or double-sided

Ribbon Measurement

- **Short:** 8RW

- **Medium:** 10RW

- **Long:** 12RW

*See the Ribbon Cutting
Chart (page 17).*

DIRECTIONS

*See General Instructions
(page 28).*

1. Cut 1 length of
ribbon. Fold the length
in half; insert a pin at the
fold. Fold each raw edge
behind the ribbon to
the pin; overlap the raw
edges. Re-pin to hold.

2. Anchor knot the
thread into the selvage
edge at the pin. Gather
stitch through all of the
layers of ribbon. Pull in
the gathers; tackstitch
and anchor knot the
thread.

Finished leaf

Regal Leaf

Group of Regal Leaves

SKILL LEVEL: *Intermediate* ◕◕

Suggested Ribbon

Woven or French wire ribbon with soft or medium hand, single- or double-sided

Ribbon Measurement

▪ 12RW

See the Ribbon Cutting Chart (page 17).

DIRECTIONS

See General Instructions (page 28) and Elizabethan Leaf, Petal, or Bud (page 125).

1. Cut 2 lengths of ribbon 12RW. Working with the first length, follow the directions for the Elizabethan Leaf. Repeat for the other length.

2. Tackstitch the raw edges together.

Finished leaf

Kimono Calyx and Bud

Kimono Calyx over Kimono Bud

SKILL LEVEL: *Intermediate* ◕◕

Suggested Ribbon

2 different colors of woven or French wire ribbon with soft or medium hand, single- or double-sided

Ribbon Measurement

▪ **Bud:** 4RW

▪ **Calyx:** 4RW

See the Ribbon Cutting Chart (page 17).

DIRECTIONS

See General Assembly Directions (page 121) and Kimono Leaf, Petal, or Bud (page 124).

1. Bud: Cut 1 length of ribbon 4RW. Follow the directions for the kimono petal/bud; keep the needle threaded, and do not anchor or cut the thread.

2. Calyx: Cut 1 length of ribbon 4RW. Place the bud in the center of the wrong side of the length. Tackstitch the bud to the calyx.

3. Follow the folding and stitching directions for the kimono leaf.

Finished calyx over bud

Bud Cap

Bud Cap and Petals

SKILL LEVEL: *Intermediate* 🌢🌢

Suggested Ribbon

Woven or French wire ribbon with soft or medium hand, single- or double-sided

Additional Supplies

Second threaded needle

Ribbon Measurement

- 6RW

See the Ribbon Cutting Chart (page 17).

DIRECTIONS

See General Instructions (page 28) and Woven and Silk Bias Berries (page 149). Use the bud cap on a coneflower, vine flower, fuchsia, or any of the individual-petal flowers to create a side-view flower.

1. Cut 1 length of ribbon 6RW. Follow the directions for the woven berry through the gather stitching on the outer edge; keep the needle threaded, and do not anchor or cut the thread.

2. Using the second needle, anchor knot the thread through the raw edges of the flower and then insert through the center of the bud cap; pull the raw edges of the petals into the cap. Stitch the needle back through the cap. Anchor knot the thread into the raw edges of the petals; cut the thread.

3. Pull the thread of the bud cap tight to close around the raw edges of the petals. Tackstitch around the outer edge of the cap through the petals.

4. Anchor knot the thread into the ditch of the seam in the bud cap.

Finished bud cap with petals

Simple Calyx

Simple Calyx

SKILL LEVEL: *Easy* 🌢

Suggested Ribbon

Woven ribbon with soft, medium, or stiff hand, single- or double-sided

Ribbon Measurement

- **Soft hand:** 7RW
- **Medium hand:** 8RW
- **Stiff hand:** 9RW

See the Ribbon Cutting Chart (page 17).

DIRECTIONS

See General Instructions (page 28) and Rosette (page 35).

Cut 1 length of ribbon. Follow the assembly and stitching directions for the rosette. Stitch or glue the rosette to the wrong side of a flower or corsage to cover the raw edges.

Finished flower with calyx

Morning Glory Leaf

Morning Glory Leaf

SKILL LEVEL: *Easy* 🌢

Suggested Ribbon

Silk bias ribbon: habotai, satin, or velvet

Ribbon Measurement

■ 3RW

See the Ribbon Cutting Chart (page 17).

DIRECTIONS

See General Assembly Directions (page 121).

1. Cut 1 length of ribbon 3RW. Fold and gently finger-press the width of the ribbon in half, wrong sides in. Fold the length of the ribbon in half to create a second fold; match the raw edges. Insert a pin 1RW from the raw edges.

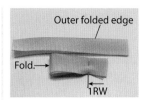

2. Anchor knot the thread into the bias edges at the second fold. Gather stitch through the layers of ribbon to the pin; curve the stitches slightly to ⅛″ in from the outer folded and raw edges.

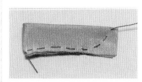

3. Gently pull in the gathers to form the leaf. Tackstitch and anchor knot the thread into the raw edges.

Finished leaf

Rounded Leaf

Group of Rounded Leaves

SKILL LEVEL: *Easy* 🌢

Suggested Ribbon

Silk bias ribbon: habotai, satin, or velvet

Ribbon Measurement

■ Short: 3RW

■ Medium: 5RW

See the Ribbon Cutting Chart (page 17).

DIRECTIONS

See General Instructions (page 28).

1. Cut 1 length of ribbon. Fold the ribbon length in half, right side in; match the raw edges. Use assembly stitch 2 to stitch the raw edges together with a ⅛″ seam allowance. Anchor knot the thread into the bias edges.

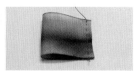

2. Fold and gently finger-press the width of the ribbon in half, right side out. Anchor knot the 2 raw edges of ribbon together at the seam.

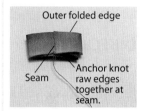

3. Arrange the ribbon with the seam at one end and a fold at the opposite end. Gather stitch through all the layers of ribbon from the seam to the fold at the opposite end.

4. Gently pull in the gathers to form the leaf. Tackstitch and anchor knot the thread into the bias edges.

Finished leaf

Double-Edge Leaf

Group of Double-Edge Leaves

Suggested Ribbon

Silk bias habotai ribbon

Ribbon Measurement

- **Short:** 3RW

- **Medium:** 5RW

See the Ribbon Cutting Chart (page 17).

DIRECTIONS

See General Instructions (page 28).

1. Cut 1 length of ribbon. Fold and gently finger-press the width of the ribbon to ⅝ the original width. Fold the ribbon length in half, right side in, to form a second fold; match the raw edges. Insert a pin 1RW (the new folded width) from the raw edges.

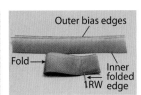

2. Anchor knot the thread on the outer bias edge ⅛" in from the raw edges. Gather stitch diagonally toward where the pin meets the folded edge; loop over the folded edge. Continue gather stitching along the folded edges to the second fold.

3. Gently pull in the gathers to form the leaf. Tackstitch and anchor knot the thread into the folded edges.

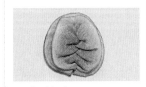

Finished leaf

Pointed Leaf

Group of Pointed Leaves

Suggested Ribbon

Silk bias ribbon: habotai, satin, or velvet

Ribbon Measurement

- **Short:** 3RW

- **Medium:** 5RW

See the Ribbon Cutting Chart (page 17).

DIRECTIONS

See General Instructions page 28) and Rounded Leaf (page 137).

1. Cut 1 length of ribbon. Follow Steps 1 and 2 for the rounded leaf. Arrange the ribbon with the seam at one end and a fold at the opposite end. Insert a pin 1RW in from the folded width.

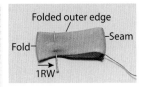

2. Gather stitch through all the layers of ribbon from the seam to the pin.

3. Gently pull in the gathers to form the leaf. Tackstitch and anchor knot the thread into the bias edges. Using assembly stitch 1, stitch diagonally to the fold; stitch back to the bias edges; anchor knot the thread into the bias edges.

Finished leaf

Garden Extras

The following designs can be used to enhance your floral vignettes.
Many of the designs require very little yardage, giving you an excellent
opportunity to use those tiny bits of leftover ribbon.

Country Heart ... 140
½" satin ribbon

Fan ... 140
⅜" woven ribbon

Double Fan ... 141
⅝" double-sided satin ribbon

Garden Snail ... 141
⅜" single-sided satin ribbon

Gwen's Butterfly ... 142
⅜" single- and double-sided satin ribbons

Summer's Dragonfly ... 143
⅜" single-sided satin ribbon

Shutterbug Center and Button ... 144
⅜" satin ribbon

Simple Bow ... 145
⅜" satin ribbon

Ribbon Button ... 145
⅜" double-sided satin ribbon

Shy Butterfly ... 146
2 colors of ⅜" woven ribbon

Elegant Heart ... 147
½" satin ribbon

Looped Plume ... 148
⅜" double-sided satin ribbon

Half U-Gather Petals ... 148
½" satin ribbon

Woven and Silk Bias Berries ... 149
⅞" satin ribbon (fuchsia), ⅝" silk bias ribbon (red), ¾" satin ribbon (purple, stuffed), and ⅝" silk bias ribbon (red, stuffed)

GENERAL DIRECTIONS

See General Instructions (page 28).

A few of these techniques are used to create a portion of another design. If the measurements differ, use those given for the design you are constructing.

Ribbon Measurement

Each set of directions will give an RW measurement length to cut the ribbon for the design; use the Ribbon Cutting Chart (page 17) to find the correct measurement for the specific ribbon width you have selected.

Country Heart

Country Heart

SKILL LEVEL: *Easy* 🞈

Suggested Ribbon

Woven or French wire ribbon with soft, medium, or stiff hand, double-sided

Ribbon Measurement

- **Soft hand:** 8RW
- **Medium hand:** 9RW
- **Stiff hand:** 10RW

See the Ribbon Cutting Chart (page 17).

DIRECTIONS

See General Instructions (page 28).

1. Cut 1 length of ribbon according to the hand of the project ribbon. Fold the ribbon in half at an angle; place a pin through the fold.

2. Fold the ribbon length in half; match the raw edges. Using assembly stitch 2, stitch the raw edges together with a ⅛″ seam allowance. Anchor knot the thread into the raw edges.

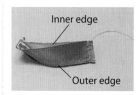

Inner edge

Outer edge

3. Stitch into the inner selvage edge next to the seam; gather stitch along the selvage edge, the folds, and the remaining selvage edge; loop over the edges. Gently pull the thread to form the lobes. Tackstitch and anchor knot the thread into the raw edges.

Finished Country Heart

Fan

Fan

SKILL LEVEL: *Easy* 🞈

Suggested Ribbon

Woven or French wire ribbon with soft or medium hand, single- or double-sided

Ribbon Measurement

- **6RW**

See the Ribbon Cutting Chart (page 17).

DIRECTIONS

See General Instructions (page 28) and Posy (page 38).

1. Cut 1 length of ribbon 6RW. Follow the pinning and gather-stitch directions for the posy.

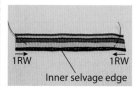

1RW   1RW

Inner selvage edge

2. Gently pull the thread to form the center; line up the raw edges side by side. Tackstitch and anchor knot the thread into the raw edges.

Keep raw edges below gathers.

Finished Fan

Double Fan

Double Fan

Suggested Ribbon

Woven or French wire ribbon with soft or medium hand, double-sided

Ribbon Measurement

■ 9RW

See the Ribbon Cutting Chart (page 17).

DIRECTIONS

See General Instructions (page 28) and Two-Petal Flower (page 42).

1. Cut 1 length of ribbon 9RW. Follow the pinning and gather-stitch directions for the two-petal flower, measuring 4RW for each petal.

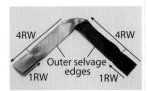

2. Gently pull the thread to form the 2 lobes; match the raw edges side by side. Tackstitch and anchor knot the thread into the raw edges.

Finished Double Fan

Garden Snail

Garden Snail

Suggested Ribbon

Woven ribbon with soft or medium hand, single- or double-sided

Additional Supplies

■ 1 folded stamen

Ribbon Measurement

■ 8RW

See the Ribbon Cutting Chart (page 17).

DIRECTIONS

See General Instructions (page 28) and Posy (page 38).

1. Cut 1 length of ribbon 8RW. Follow the pinning and gather-stitch directions for the posy up to the last pin.

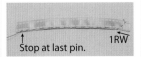

Stop at last pin.   1RW

2. Fold under the raw edge 1RW. Pin to hold.

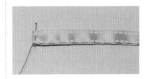

3. Pull the thread to form the body. Tackstitch the thread into the raw edge next to the beginning anchor knot.

4. Stitch the folded edge using assembly stitch 1. Tackstitch the stamen to the raw edges; anchor knot and cut the thread.

Finished Garden Snail

Gwen's Butterfly

Gwen's Butterfly

SKILL LEVEL: *Intermediate* ◗◗

Suggested Ribbon

2 different colors of the same width of woven or French wire ribbon with soft or medium hand, double-sided

Additional Supplies

- 2 folded stamens

Ribbon Measurement

- **Wings:** 9RW (Cut 2.)
- **Body:** 8RW

See the Ribbon Cutting Chart (page 17).

DIRECTIONS

See General Instructions (page 28), Two-Petal Flower (page 42), and Iris Leaf (page 131).

1. Wings: Cut 2 lengths of ribbon 9RW. Follow the pinning and gather-stitch directions for the two-petal flower, measuring 4RW for each side. Repeat for the other length; fold the 2 lengths in opposite directions.

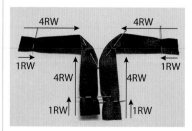

2. Gently pull the thread on the first length to form a set of wings; line up the raw edges side by side. Tackstitch and anchor knot the thread into the raw edges. Repeat for the other set of wings. Tackstitch the raw edges of the 2 groups of wings together.

3. Fold 1 stamen for the antennae and 1 for the legs. Tackstitch these on top of the raw edges of the wings.

Tackstitch antennae and legs to wings.

4. Body: Cut 1 length of ribbon 8RW. Follow the directions for the iris leaf.

5. Whipstitch the body over the raw edges of the wings and stamens.

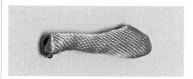

Finished Gwen's Butterfly

Summer's Dragonfly

Summer's Dragonfly

SKILL LEVEL: *Intermediate* ● ●

Suggested Ribbon

3 different colors of the same width of woven ribbon with soft or medium hand, single- or double-sided

Additional Supplies

■ Second threaded needle

Ribbon Measurement

■ **Wings:** 8RW (Cut 2.);
    6RW (Cut 2.)

■ **Body:** 8RW

See the Ribbon Cutting Chart (page 17).

DIRECTIONS

See General Instructions (page 28), Spear-Tip Leaf, Petal, or Bud (page 126), and Iris Leaf (page 131).

1. Wings: Cut 2 lengths of ribbon 8RW and 2 lengths of ribbon 6RW. Follow the directions for the spear-tip petal for each length; cut off the thread.

2. Body: Cut 1 length of ribbon 8RW. Follow the directions for the iris leaf; do not cut the thread.

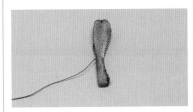

3. Using the second needle, tackstitch the raw edges of 1 small and 1 large wing together; cut the thread.

4. Insert the raw edges through the middle of the body. Repeat Step 3 for the other set of wings. Using the second needle, tackstitch these to the first set; cut the thread.

Tackstitch raw edges of wing sets together.

5. Center the body over the wings to cover the stitching. Using the thread from the body, tackstitch the back of the body to the wings; cut the thread.

Back of body

Finished Summer's Dragonfly

Shutterbug Center and Button

Shutterbug Center

SKILL LEVEL: *Easy* 🌢

Suggested Ribbon

Woven ribbon with soft or medium hand, double-sided

Ribbon Measurement

- **Center:** 3RW (Cut 3.)
- **Button:** 2RW (Cut 3.)

See the Ribbon Cutting Chart (page 17).

DIRECTIONS

See General Instructions (page 28).

1. Center: Cut 3 lengths of ribbon 3RW. Overlap and align the raw edge of the first length with the selvage edge of the next length, right sides up. Insert a pin through both layers. Repeat this for the remaining length, overlapping the last length over the first.

2. Anchor knot the thread into a corner section, 1RW in from the selvage edge. Gather stitch at an angle through both layers of ribbon across the corner section toward the opposite selvage edge; loop over the edge. Gather stitch along the selvage edges and across the corner sections; loop over each edge. Continue back to the beginning anchor knot.

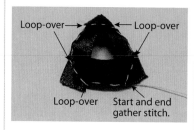

Loop-over → ← Loop-over

Loop-over   Start and end gather stitch.

3. Pull the thread tight to form the center. Tackstitch the raw edges together and anchor knot the thread.

Finished Shutterbug Center

4. Button: Cut 3 lengths of ribbon 2RW. Repeat Step 1.

5. Repeat Steps 2 and 3.

Finished Shutterbug Button

Simple Bow

Simple Bow

SKILL LEVEL: **Easy** 🌢

Suggested Ribbon

Woven or French wire ribbon with soft or medium hand, double-sided

Ribbon Measurement

- Bow: 6RW
- Knot: 12RW

See the Ribbon Cutting Chart (page 17).

DIRECTIONS

See General Instructions (page 28), Shy Butterfly (page 146), and Knot Center (page 122).

1. Bow: Cut 1 length of ribbon 6RW. Follow the folding and gather-stitch directions for 1 wing of the shy butterfly.

Whipstitch around the gathered middle. Anchor knot and cut the thread.

2. Knot: Cut 1 length of ribbon 12RW. Tie an overhand knot over the stitches of the bow. Note that the knot is tied in the back.

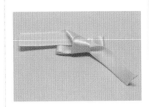

Finished Simple Bow

Ribbon Button

Ribbon Button

SKILL LEVEL: *Intermediate* 🌢🌢

Suggested Ribbon

Woven or French wire ribbon with soft, medium, or stiff hand, double-sided

Ribbon Measurement

- 13RW

See the Ribbon Cutting Chart (page 17).

DIRECTIONS

See General Instructions (page 28).

1. Cut 1 length of ribbon 13RW. Fold the ribbon at a 45° angle, with the left side of the ribbon over the right.

2. Fold the bottom ribbon over the top ribbon and flush with the left selvage edge. Tackstitch the corner.

3. Fold the bottom ribbon over the top ribbon.

4. Continue to fold the bottom ribbon over the top ribbon until you have 5 sections. Tuck the raw edges to the wrong side; trim any excess ribbon and tackstitch through the last corner.

Tuck raw edges to wrong side.

5. Tackstitch and anchor knot the thread into the raw edges.

Finished Ribbon Button

Shy Butterfly

Shy Butterfly

SKILL LEVEL: *Easy* 🌰

Suggested Ribbon

2 different colors of the same width of woven or French wire ribbon with soft or medium hand, single- or double-sided

Additional Supplies

- 1 folded stamen
- 2 strands of cotton floss

Ribbon Measurement

- **Top wings:** 7RW
- **Bottom wings:** 6RW

See the Ribbon Cutting Chart (page 17).

DIRECTIONS

See General Instructions (page 28).

1. Cut 1 length of ribbon 7RW and 1 length of ribbon 6RW. Fold a length of ribbon in half, wrong side in, to find the center. Fold each raw edge toward the center; overlap the raw edges ⅛"; insert a pin through all layers of ribbon. Repeat for the other length to make 2 sets of wings. Note that the raw edges are the back of the butterfly.

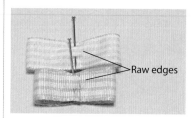

Raw edges

2. Anchor knot the thread into the selvage edges of the shorter set of wings (these will be the bottom wings). Gather stitch through the raw edges and all layers of both sets of wings.

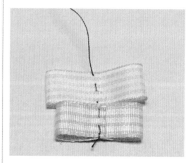

3. Pull the thread slightly to gather the middle of the wings. Anchor knot the thread at the outer selvage edge of the longer, top set of wings.

4. Place the stamen over the gathered stitches on the right side of the wings. Whipstitch over the stamen with 2 strands of floss.

Whipstitch stamen over gathered stitches.

Finished Shy Butterfly

Elegant Heart

Elegant Heart

SKILL LEVEL: *Advanced* ●●●

Suggested Ribbon

Woven or French wire ribbon with soft, medium, or stiff hand, single- or double-sided

Ribbon Measurement

- Soft hand: 8RW
- Medium hand: 9RW
- Stiff hand: 10RW

See the Ribbon Cutting Chart (page 17).

DIRECTIONS

See General Instructions (page 28) and Lance Leaf (page 127).

1. Cut 1 length of ribbon. Follow Step 1 of the lance leaf directions. Stitch through the fold using assembly stitch 2.

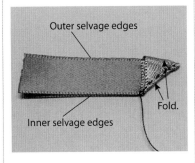

Outer selvage edges

Inner selvage edges

Fold.

2. Open the ribbon and insert a pin 1RW from each raw edge.

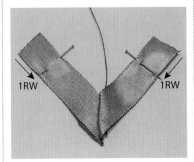

1RW

1RW

3. For the first petal, gather stitch along the inner selvage edge to the pin; loop over the edge. Gather stitch diagonally toward the point that is ⅛" in from the outer selvage and raw edge. Gently pull the thread to form the first lobe; keep the raw edges on the same side as the lobe. Tackstitch the raw edges to the fold; anchor knot the thread.

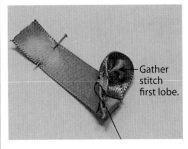

Gather stitch first lobe.

4. Repeat Step 3 for the other lobe.

Gather stitch second lobe.

Finished Elegant Heart

Looped Plume

Looped Plume

SKILL LEVEL: *Easy* 🌢

Suggested Ribbon

Woven or French wire ribbon with soft or medium hand, double-sided

Additional Supplies

- 2RW × 8" strip of cardstock

Ribbon Measurement

- 17½RW

See the Ribbon Cutting Chart (page 17).

DIRECTIONS

See General Instructions (page 28) and Bias-Loop Petals (page 46).

1. Cut 1 length of ribbon 17½RW. Follow the looping and gather-stitch directions for the bias-loop petals.

2. Pull the thread to gather the ribbon. Tackstitch and anchor knot the thread into the raw edges.

Finished Looped Plume

Half U-Gather Petals

Half U-Gather Petal

SKILL LEVEL: *Easy* 🌢

Suggested Ribbon

Woven ribbon with soft or medium hand, single- or double-sided

Ribbon Measurement

- 4RW

See the Ribbon Cutting Chart (page 17).

DIRECTIONS

See General Instructions (page 28).

1. Cut 1 length of ribbon 4RW. Fold the ribbon length in half, right side in. Anchor knot the thread into the selvage edges at the fold.

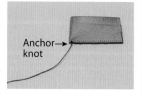

Anchor→ knot

2. Gather stitch through both layers of ribbon, diagonally and on a slight curve, toward the point that is ⅛" in from the outer selvage and the raw edges.

End gather stitch.
←1RW
Start gather stitch.

3. Gently pull the thread to form the center. Tackstitch and anchor knot the thread into the raw edges.

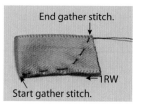

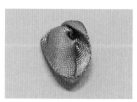

Finished petal

Woven and Silk Bias Berries

Woven and Silk Bias Berries, and Stuffed Berries

SKILL LEVEL: *Easy* ◆

Suggested Ribbon

▪ **Woven berry:** Woven or French wire ribbon with soft or medium hand, single- or double-sided

▪ **Bias berry:** Silk bias habotai, satin, or silk velvet ribbon, single- or double-sided

Note that the inner selvage edge will be the top of the berry and the outer selvage edge will be the bottom.

Additional Supplies

▪ Small amount of batting for stuffed berries

Ribbon Measurement

▪ Woven berry: 4RW

▪ Bias berry: 3RW

▪ Stuffed woven berry: 6RW

▪ Stuffed bias berry: 4RW

See the Ribbon Cutting Chart (page 17).

DIRECTIONS

See General Instructions (page 28) and Rosette (page 35). Where the rosette directions refer to the selvage edge, that will be the bias edge for the bias berry.

1. Cut 1 length of ribbon. Follow the seam directions for the rosette using assembly stitch 1. Follow the gather-stitch directions but pull the gathers so that they are formed on the wrong side of the ribbon. Tackstitch along the seam back to the outer selvage edge.

Outer selvage edge

2. Turn the ribbon inside out. Gather stitch along the outer selvage edge back to the beginning of the seam. If you are making the stuffed berry, roll a small amount of stuffing into a ball and insert it into the opening.

Stuffed berry

3. Gently pull the thread to close the center. Tackstitch and anchor knot the thread through the selvage edges.

Stuffed berry

Finished Berries

Finished Stuffed Berries

Gallery

VINTAGE PASTELS

Vintage Heart Wreath, 5¼" × 5½"

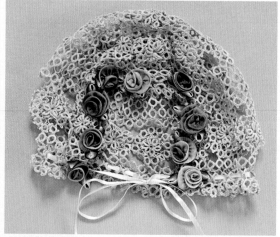

Vintage Tatted Baby's Bonnet, 5" × 5"

Vintage Gloves, 4" × 11"

COUNTRY ROADS

Morning Glories Bracelet, 1" × 6⅛"

Blue Hearts, 6½" × 5½"

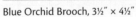

Blue Orchid Brooch, 3½" × 4½"

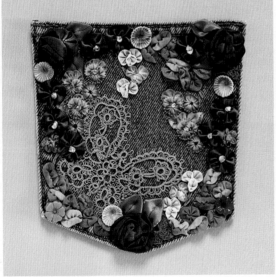

Butterflies and Snapdragons, 5¾" × 6⅛"

Spring Hydrangeas Brooch, 1¾" × 1⅛"

SUMMERTIME

Summer Wreath, 6½" × 6"

Floral Birthday Cake, 3¾" × 2¼"

Needle and Thimble Holder, 2½"

Pincushion, 2¾" × 3¾"

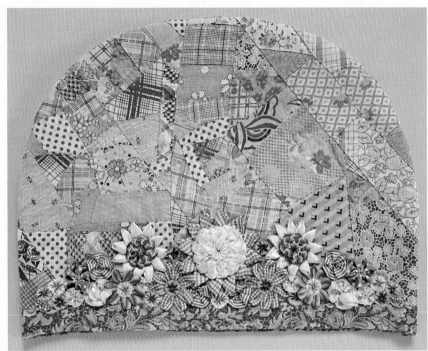

Auntie B's Tea Cozy, 11¾″ × 9″

Hotflash, 7½″ × 7½″

LATE AUTUMN ROSES

Deco Plumeria Neckpiece, 2¼″ × 19″

Indian Roses Neckpiece, 2″ × 20″

Rose Beret, 3″ × 10¼″

ENCHANTED

Daffodil Brooch, 3½″ × 2¼″

Pansy Tassel, 4″ × 16½″

Bleeding Hearts Brooch, 4″ × 3″

Red Roses Vase, 3¼″ × 5⅝″

PASSION FOR PURPLE

Fuchsia Lariat, 2″ × 22″

Violet Gardens, 3⅛″ × 2⅞″

Veronica's Violas, 4⅜″ × 2⅞″

Vintage Plums Brooch, 4½″ × 6½″

ANTIQUE ROSES

Dainty Heart Wreath, 3⅜″ × 5″

Pink Flower Reticule, 3⅛″ × 3½″

Floral Hatbox,
3½″ wide × 2¼″ high × 4¾″ deep

Velvet Rose Corsage, 5⅜″ × 4½″

ELEGANTLY STATED

Azalea Neckpiece, 2¾" × 18"

Evening Reticule, 5¾" × 9"

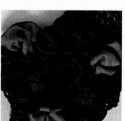

Crimson and Black: Crochet Collar, 2¾" × 24",
with Bracelet, 2⅜" × 6¾"

ABOUT THE AUTHOR

Christen Brown was born in Manhattan Beach, California, and spent her formative years in Torrance, California. She first became interested in fiber arts through making clothing for her dolls as a child. After graduating from high school, she continued her education at the Fashion Institute of Design and Merchandising in Los Angeles, California, where she graduated with an AA in fashion design. She is interested in craft and fine art, and continues to experiment and learn in the area of design in general, specifically in the techniques of embroidery, quilting, ribbonwork, and jewelry making.

Christen began her career in wearable art in 1986. Her work has been shown in galleries and fashion shows all over the world. She has been invited on multiple occasions to participate in both the Fairfield and Bernina fashion shows. Her work has been included in *The Costume-Maker's Art, The Button Lover's Book, Michaels Create!* magazine, *Martha Stewart Weddings* magazine, and *Visions: Quilts of a New Decade,* to name but a few.

Christen is now concentrating on writing and publishing her work. She has written several articles for *PieceWork* magazine, a publication that explores the history of needlework. She has also been published in *Threads* magazine.

Having already had a remarkable journey through life, Christen has set several goals for the future—to continually be inspired, to be creative, to be necessary. She works and teaches out of her home studio in San Diego, California, and teaches several times a year for an online art site.

Visit the author at her website:
www.christenbrown.com.

Great Titles and Tools

from C&T PUBLISHING and stashBOOKS.

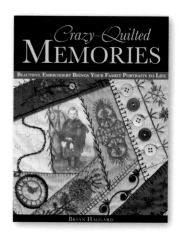

Available at your local retailer or **www.ctpub.com** *or* **800-284-1114**

For a list of other fine books from C&T Publishing, visit our website to view our catalog online.

C&T PUBLISHING, INC.

P.O. Box 1456
Lafayette, CA 94549
800-284-1114

Email: ctinfo@ctpub.com
Website: www.ctpub.com

C&T Publishing's professional photography services are now available to the public. Visit us at www.ctmediaservices.com.

Tips and Techniques can be found at www.ctpub.com > Consumer Resources > Quiltmaking Basics: Tips & Techniques for Quiltmaking & More

For quilting supplies:

COTTON PATCH

1025 Brown Ave.
Lafayette, CA 94549
Store: 925-284-1177
Mail order: 925-283-7883

Email: CottonPa@aol.com
Website: www.quiltusa.com

Note: Fabrics shown may not be currently available, as fabric manufacturers keep most fabrics in print for only a short time.